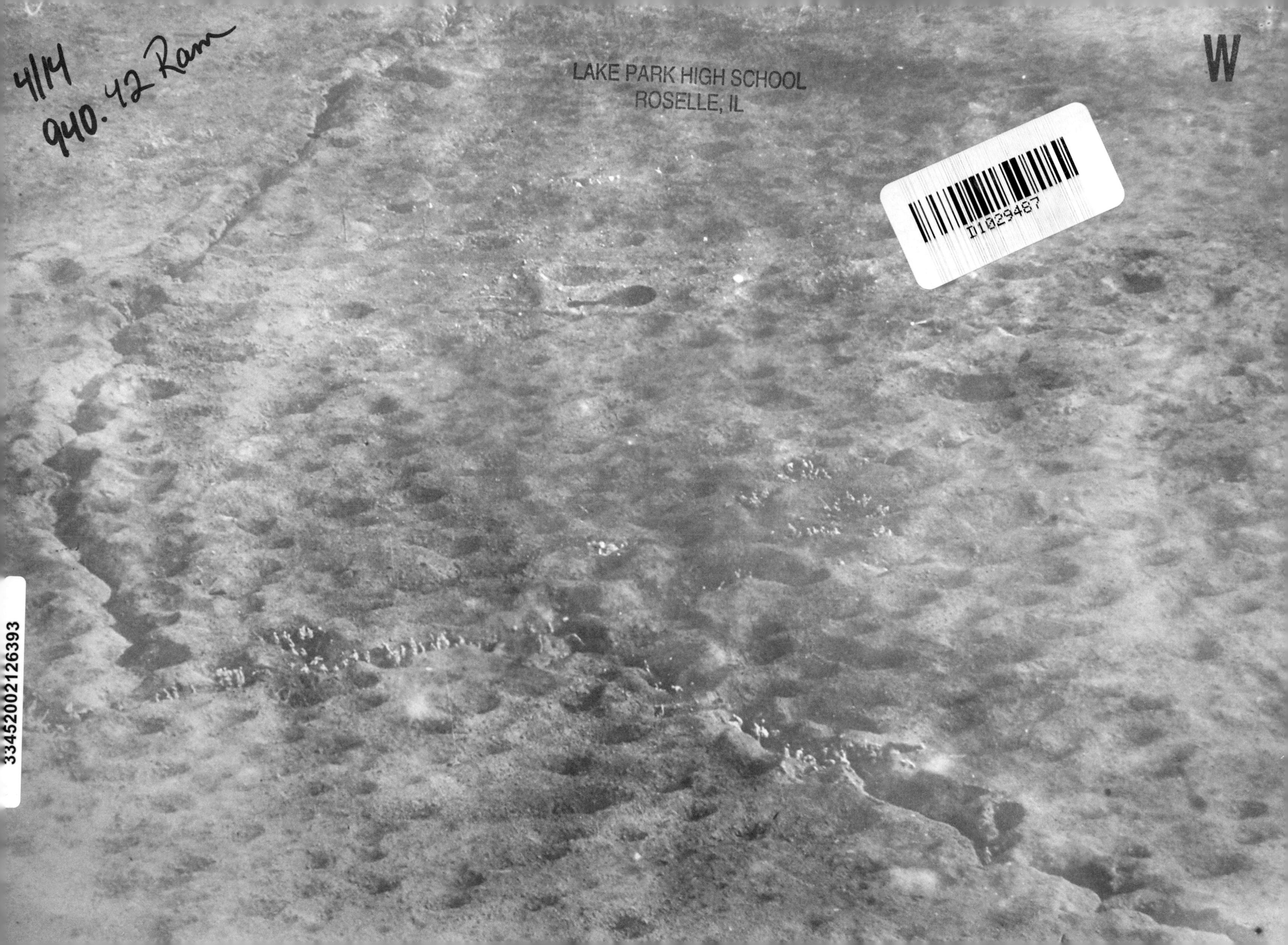

THE GREAT WAR
FROM THE AIR
THEN AND NOW

Gail Ramsey (*Καλλιοπη Μακρη*)

LAKE PARK HIGH SCHOOL
ROSELLE, IL

*How senseless is everything that can ever be written, done, or thought,
when such things are possible. It must be all lies and of no account when
the culture of a thousand years could not prevent this stream of blood
being poured out, these torture-chambers in their hundreds of thousands.
A hospital alone shows what war is.*

ERICH MARIA REMARQUE
All Quiet on the Western Front, 1929

Credits

ISBN: 9 781870 067812

© *After the Battle*/Gail Ramsey 2013

Designed by Winston G. Ramsey, Editor-in-Chief *After the Battle*

PUBLISHERS
Battle of Britain International Ltd., Hobbs Cross House, Old Harlow, Essex CM17 0NN

PRINTERS
Printed and bound by Ozgraf S. A., Olsztyn, Poland

FRONT COVER
A montage of reconnaissance photographs overlaid on the trench map used for the attack mounted at Fromelles in July 1916.

REAR COVER
Hooge Crater Cemetery, originally with 76 graves, now with 2,345.

ENDPAPERS
Front: These striking French low-level oblique photographs show the front-line Tranchée Guillaume south of Vermandovillers *(left)* as it appeared on September 17, 1916, and Tranchée des Gémaux *(right)* just west of Soyécourt on October 10, 1916.

Rear: Save for one day in October 1914, Ypres managed to remain in British hands throughout the war although it received a severe battering from German artillery which began in November. Barrages continued in 1915 during the Second Battle of Ypres and again during the Third Battle in 1917. The magnificent Cloth Hall took over 40 years to be reconstructed only being completed in 1967.

PHOTOGRAPHIC CREDITS
After the Battle 4, 6, 8, 9 right, 10 left, 18 right, 20, 23, 25 left, 27 left, 28, 53 left, 54 left, 60 right, 61 left, 72 right, 73 left, 8 inset, 88, 94, 98, 100, 102, 107 left, 108, 112 top right, 116, 118 top, 120, 123 top right. **Canadian War Museum** 92 top. **Chris Weeks** 7 right. **Commonwealth War Graves Commission** 7 left. **Ed Storey** 111 left. **Imperial War Museum** 10 right (Q45960), 33 inset (Q64641), 38 (Q55066), 48 (Q37465), 51 inset (Q57703), 56 (Q61475), 58 (Q58141), 62 inset (Q37744), 70 left (HU91107), 71 right (HU91108), 74 (Q57677), 79 top right (Q58378), 82 left (Q41961), 90 right (Q47847), 103 left (Q44808), 104 (Q85216), 108 inset (Q42917), 113 left (Q17255), 114 right (Q42050). **Jean Paul Pallud** 34. **John Giles** 40 left, 65 centre, 83 top right. **Service Historique de la Défense, Vincinnes** Front Endpapers, 30, 36, 37, 45 top left and right, 67 top left, 76, 78 left, 84, 86 left, 87 top, 119 top, 122, 124, 126. The Google Earth views are reproduced under licence.

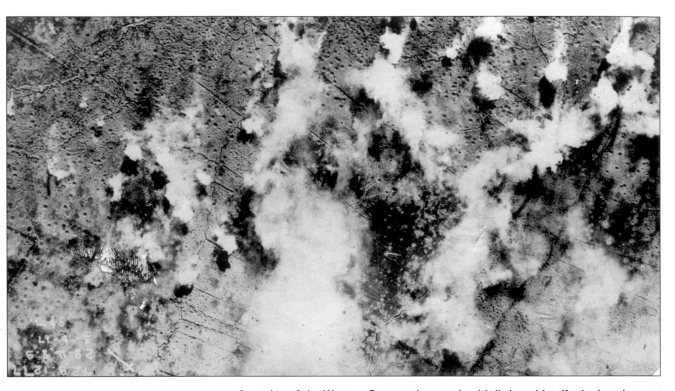

A section of the Western Front under attack with little to identify the location, yet the devastation caused to huge swathes of countryside is self-evident. This book shows how the land has been transformed over the last hundred years.

Contents

Designed by Sir Reginald Blomfield, the Menin Gate Memorial to the Missing at Ypres was begun in 1923 but not inaugurated by Field-Marshal Herbert Plumer until July 24, 1927.

On a balmy evening, standing under the majestic Menin Gate Memorial to the Missing in Ypres, I wait in anticipation. Every evening at 8 p.m. the road is closed and buglers from the local fire brigade sound the Last Post, the ceremony having taken place since July 1, 1928. Despite its cessation during German occupation in the Second World War, it recommenced on the very evening that Polish troops liberated Ypres in 1944. As others I am sure have felt over the many years that visitors have stood quietly and paid tribute, I am humbled by both the scale of the sacrifice represented in the 54,896 names engraved on this memorial to those with no known grave, and equally by the devotion of the locals with this daily act of remembrance.

My thoughts drift to the cemeteries that I visited nearby that day with their manicured lawns and white headstones gleaming in the midday sun, and the battlefields once pitted with shell holes, now tranquil fields of crops awaiting harvest. What a striking contrast this vision is to the hell on earth that the men commemorated on the memorial and those buried in the many cemeteries across the Western Front would have experienced. Over 8,500,000 men from Great Britain and its Empire served of whom nearly a million lost their lives. Just over half — 588,972 — are buried in named graves, but a further 187,644 were never identified, interred in graves simply marked 'Known unto God'. All of this difficult to comprehend in the light of modern conflict, but for the men on the ground at that time the then-new technologies of aviation and photography became paramount to their survival and success.

It has not been my intention in this book to give another account of the war itself as that has been done before many times by many authors. Instead I wanted to present a bird's-eye view of the battlefield . . . as it was then and as it appears today. By the end of the war the once peaceful countryside of Belgium and France had suffered years of attrition, whole swathes having been pounded into dust — or rather mud — yet over the past century man and nature have combined to assuage the worst of the destruction as the present-day photography shows.

Wartime photographs taken at ground level can only show the damage from one dimension but aerial photographs give a much larger view and add a different perspective. Only on seeing the scale of the shelling that the aerial photographs demonstrate can one begin to comprehend the extensive loss of life and property damage that took place across Belgium and France. As these images combine to build a mosaic of the front line areas, they reveal the intricate trench networks used by both sides as the vast peppered landscape unfolds before us.

Despite photography and aviation both being relatively in their infancy, the men who risked their lives taking the aerial photographs have left us a wonderful legacy. This was strikingly demonstrated in 2008 when the examination of aerial photos directly led to the discovery of 250 missing Allied soldiers in mass graves at Fromelles (see page 60). Using DNA samples, many of the dead were then successfully identified and given named graves in Pheasant Wood Military Cemetery.

Yet it still remains a sobering thought that the remains of over 300,000 Allied fighting men still lay undiscovered on the battlefield. Aerial photographs, used alongside today's technology, could well be the key to locating many of our missing men still lying in unmarked graves.

GAIL RAMSEY, 2013

For more information on the memorials, cemeteries and museums that now cover the Western Front, readers may find it helpful to consult our sister publication Before Endeavours Fade. Having repeatedly visited the battlefields over a period of 50 years, the late Miss Rose Coombs was second to none as a source for the minutia of the First World War.

ACKNOWLEDGEMENTS

First and foremost for his wonderful support, advice and encouragement, I thank my husband Winston Ramsey. And, as with every *After the Battle* publication, the hard work and good spirit of Rob Green was invaluable. Also for their expert assistance I thank Jean Paul Pallud, Karel Margry and Ed Storey. Finally for their continued love and support from across the world, many thanks to my family and friends in Australia.

DEDICATION

This book is dedicated to my grandfather Emanuel Makris, 1893-1963.

Introduction

The war of 1914-1918 — the 'Great War' as it was called at the time — left huge swathes of northern France and western Belgium almost totally destroyed. George B. Ford, an American town planner who travelled the area soon after the war, wrote in 1919 that 'so stupendous is the destruction in the devastated regions of France that no-one can begin to realise what it means. It is only by travelling day after day in an automobile through village after village and town after town, often where nothing is standing erect more than a few feet above the ground, that one can begin to have any conception of its enormousness'.

The Royal Regiment of Artillery alone had fired not far short of a thousand million rounds just from its 18-pdrs, so when added to the French 75mms and the German 77mms, and the really big guns on both sides, the destruction wrought by shell-fire was immeasurable. The ground had been churned into miles of water-filled shell-holes; complete villages had been razed to the ground, and every forest blown to pieces. The former rich arable land was not only pulverised but was now contaminated with the detritus of war. Trenches. . . dugouts . . . thousands of miles of barbed wire . . . abandoned equipment . . . the smashed remains of hundreds of thousands of horses and men . . . the unexploded shells; all of this created an indescribable landscape.

Once the Armistice had been signed in November 1918, the politicians focussed on the forthcoming peace negotiations to be held at Versailles and the level of reparations to be paid by Germany to rebuild that which had been destroyed. To this end, French army engineers had already been instructed to survey each commune. Maps were then prepared using three different tints to specify the level of destruction: simple debris clearance; considerable restoration, or totally devastated.

In the least damaged zone at the rear (coloured blue), prisoners of war were already working on clearing up to bring the land back to production as soon as possible. As the next Yellow Zone — a band roughly 15 kilometres wide — would require the removal of all war matériel and all trenches and shell-holes to be back-filled, it was realised that this task might well take a number of years.

The Red Zone, also some 10-15 kilometres wide, encompassed the very worst of the front line. Here, there was absolute total destruction where every building had been ground into dust, and the actual earth itself had been so mixed with the substrate that restitution would be a long and costly job. Some even debated that the Red Zone could never be brought back to use and should be abandoned to nature. In France alone this covered nearly 50,000 acres, probably the most severe département being the Aisne where there was not a single village left standing.

As farmers returned to their land, the conditions they found were awful. Not only was there no habitation but fruit trees and vineyards had simply disappeared; livestock was non-existent as was fodder, and there was no seed to plant or even machinery to level the land.

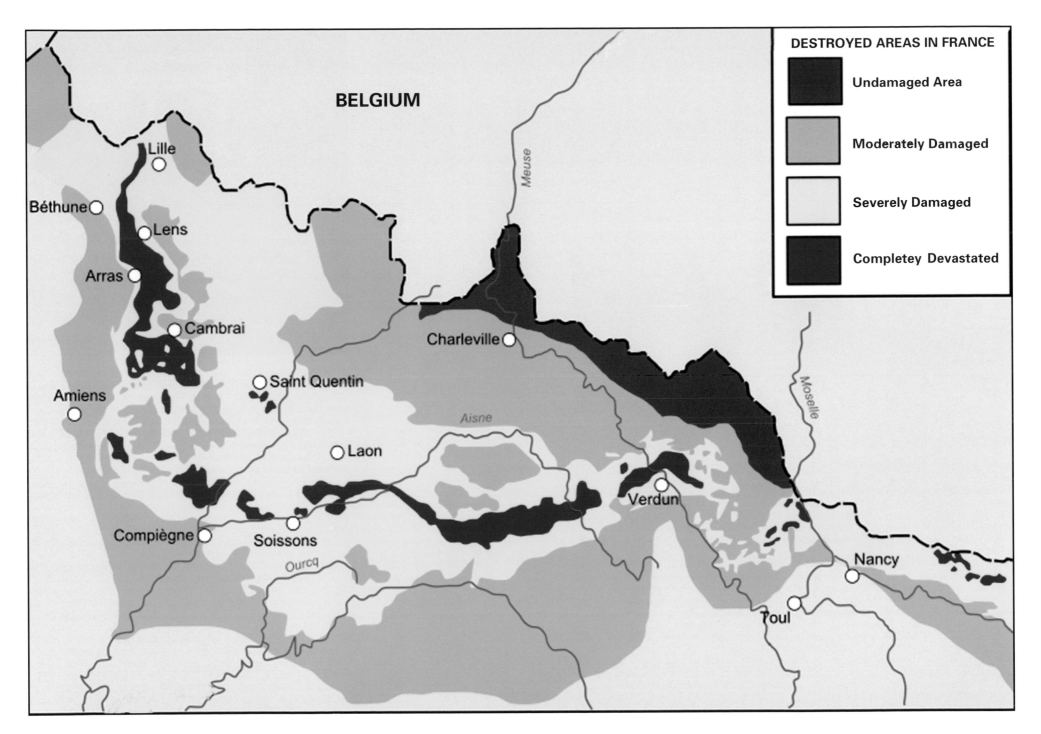

DESTROYED AREAS IN FRANCE

- Undamaged Area
- Moderately Damaged
- Severely Damaged
- Completey Devastated

BELGIUM

Lille
Béthune
Lens
Arras
Cambrai
Amiens
Saint Quentin
Charleville
Laon
Verdun
Compiègne
Soissons
Nancy
Toul

Meuse
Moselle
Aisne
Ourcq

Left: **These were the instruments of war that created the battlefield wasteland. The British shells illustrated here are the 15-inch Howitzer Mk1, 12-inch Howitzer Mk1, 9.2-inch Howitzer Mk2, 8-inch Howitzer Mk7, 6-inch 30cwt Howitzer Mk1, 5-inch Howitzer Mk1, 60-pdr Mk2, 4.5-inch Howitzer Mk2.** *Above:* **At the end of the 1920s, millions of tons of shells were still being recovered each year and today, a hundred years later, the so-called 'iron harvest' is still claiming lives to add to the total of those who died during the war.**

Then there were railways and their stations to rebuild; roads, bridges and tunnels to restore; canals to repair, and coal mines to bring back into working order. Whole towns and villages had to be rebuilt from the ground up and industry restarted but nevertheless George Ford commented that there was 'a very general feeling that almost everyone will return to the destroyed parts of the liberated regions where some 2½ million people had lived before the war'.

With such a massive task, a special ministry had been set up in France in November 1917 to plan ahead. One of the first essentials was for the provision of shelter — albeit tents and wooden army huts — and for the payment of war damage claims. Measures were also set in place for the co-ordination of the voluntary relief agencies with the civilian authorities and the army for the distribution of essential supplies of food and clothing, etc. Farming officers were appointed to liaise between farmers and the military for the provision of horses, implements and machinery, while livestock was to be provided by Germany as part of the Versailles reparations.

In December 1918, the Service des Travaux de Première Urgence (STPU) was set up in France to mastermind every facet of the restoration of the countryside using a labour force of some 80,000 French labourers and 20,000 Chinese. They were aided by 200,000 prisoners of war although after the majority had been repatriated, from 1920 they had to be replaced by workers drafted in from abroad including Poland, Portugal, Russia and Spain.

One vital aspect was for the STPU to work with the Service de Désobusage which was in charge of the disposal of ordnance, aided by British troops. As it was estimated that at least five per cent of all the shells fired had failed to explode, inevitably there were heavy casualties, not only from among the engineers charged with the clear-up, but within the civilian population, including many children, and also from the increasing number of tourists arriving to explore the battlefields who ignored the warnings.

Filling the shell-holes and trenches was also fraught with danger as machinery and tractors could strike shells with fatal results. Steam and motorised ploughs were also employed yet even when filled in, the areas continued to subside for a decade as the ground settled. Barbed wire was taken for salvage and, by the end of 1919, 222 million square metres of entanglements had been cleared. A year later over half of the trenches had been filled.

By 1922 it was recorded that over 20 million tons of munitions had been destroyed but the price was heavy: in the Pas de Calais region alone, to date 83 people had been killed and over 200 injured while undertaking the task, and there were many others who had lost their lives while working the land.

Gradually, more and more of the battlefields were being returned to agriculture and by 1930 nearly half of the farmland had been restored and was being cultivated although with mixed results due to the contamination of the soil.

From field graves to completed war cemetery. Land was ceded by the Belgian and French governments for the establishment of permanent cemeteries for the war dead. *Left:* **Three miles south-east of Ypres lay these isolated graves beside what is now Schachteweide-straat. Maple Copse was the name the Army had given to a small wood about 1,000 yards east of the village of Zillebeke. It was used by Advanced Dressing Stations and burials took** place there in June 1916 but most of the graves were destroyed in later fighting. Few graves remained marked in the cemetery which lay on the north side of the copse when this was enclosed after the Armistice. *Right:* **The cemetery now contains 308 burials but of the 78 original graves that could be located, only 26 were able to be identified. Special memorials were therefore provided to commemorate 230 casualties whose graves had been lost.**

In order to implement an orderly rebuilding programme, a law was passed in March 1919 compelling architects to produce detailed plans for the rebuilding of the villages including proposals for maintaining the character of the original. It was stressed that rebuilding could 'improve' on what was there before but not 'transform' other than the introduction of modern methods of sanitation. Much passion was raised when it was proposed to bring in craftsmen from Germany to help. While some agreed that the Germans should help rebuild what they had destroyed, others felt that they could not countenance the very idea of working alongside the former enemy.

By the mid-1920s, when most of the land in the Blue and Yellow Zones had been restored, there was more of a desire to try to redeem the Red Zone where reconstruction had been forbidden by law. However, it was appreciated that the cost would be enormous as civilian contractors would have to be brought in at commercial rates. Already the unemployed were trying to scratch a living in the Zone by stripping the copper driving bands from unexploded shells and over 20 people lost their lives so doing in 1927 alone.

It was then proposed that the state should compulsorily purchase Red Zone land from the owners but while some accepted, there were others who either refused or could not be traced. There was also the idea of delineating some locations as 'vestiges de guerre' like the Butte de Vauquois in the Meuse area and in 1928 one clever solution in the Pas de Calais was to give the war-torn land in the Red Zone at Vimy Ridge to the Canadians for a memorial.

Meanwhile, land was being gifted in perpetuity by Belgium and France for the establishment of permanent burial grounds for the dead. Great Britain and the Empire had suffered over 900,000 killed which necessitated the Imperial War Graves Commission laying out nearly 800 cemeteries — many of which were originally field cemeteries established by the Army — and by 1937 the Commission had marked 750,000 graves. Eleven Memorials to the Missing were built to commemorate those who were never found.

Americans dead totalled over 50,000 of whom only 31,000 remain buried overseas as the US Congress passed a law permitting repatriation should the next of kin wish it. The American Battle Monuments Commission was established in March 1923 to design, construct, administer and maintain eight specially-constructed burial grounds and 11 separate monuments commemorating the dead of the American Expeditionary Force.

The French recorded over 1,300,000 killed and Germany 1,800,000. Total deaths including all the other nations involved are in the region of eight million and, as Michael Clodfelter states in his *Warfare and Armed Conflicts*: 'Never in all of man's history has he seemed so intent on destroying himself as in those years between 1914 and 1918'.

At first, aerial photography was limited to the use of hand-held A-type cameras, seen here being handed to the observer of a Vickers FB5 which reached the front in 1915. Being the first specialised British fighter — the 'FB' standing for Fighting Biplane — it was armed with a single Lewis machine gun.

AERIAL PHOTOGRAPHY AND MAPPING IN WORLD WAR I

Taking photographs from the air had been experimented as far back as the 1850s using hot-air balloons but it came into its own during the First World War. Once static trench warfare began, not only was it necessary for compiling intelligence on enemy defences but it was essential for preparing suitable mapping for offensive operations.

When the British Expeditionary Force arrived on the Continent in 1914, the only topographical maps available were of a scale of 1:20,000 and 1:40,000 for Belgium and 1:80,000 in France but much larger-scale maps were essential. Photography was carried out from aircraft, static balloons, and there was even an attempt to employ cameras attached to pigeons!

The first practical use of aerial photography was in preparation for the offensive in the Artois region in March 1915. The German trench system was photographed and sketched from British and French aeroplanes enabling 1:20,000 maps to be produced before the attack by the Printing Company of the Royal Engineers. These maps were printed in several colours and an overprint (which could be updated) showed the German defences in detail. Although the British broke through the German front line on March 10 in the Battle of Neuve Chapelle, they were unable to exploit the breakthrough. Nevertheless, the experience proved that special gridded maps would be required in future so that shell-fire could be brought down accurately on enemy gun battery positions.

As time went on and the demand for maps increased, the War Office in London and Ordnance Survey in Southampton were required to help with the printing, and during the Battle of the Somme some production even had to be contracted out to printers in France.

As it was feared that maps might fall into enemy hands, at first only German trench systems were overprinted but with the absence of British trenches, this created the ridiculous situation of units having to resort to trying to capture German maps to work out where they were! Not until 1916 were the trenches of both sides shown on the same map, German defences being overprinted in red and British in blue (a reversal of the French system).

Taking photographs while leaning out of the cockpit produced oblique shots like this one of Zillebeke. This particular photograph was taken at the end of the war according to the frisket details that appear on every photograph. The devastation wrought to the Belgian countryside, with thousands of shell holes peppering the landscape is unbelievable.

As the French military had written a guide on the interpretation of air photos, this was translated into English and used until the Royal Flying Corps were able to produce their own manual in September 1916. Regular photography over the German lines allowed defence overprints to be regularly updated so that new works could be identified even if an attempt had been made at camouflage. It was equally important to mark trenches that had been abandoned.

Static observation balloons were also used, this German cameraman requiring lenses with huge magnification to be able to get close enough to photograph enemy trenches.

Between 1914 and 1918, it was estimated that over 30 million maps had been produced for the armies in France and Belgium. Very few survive today, and if and when they become available, they are very expensive. However, more than 700 have been digitised and are now available on disk from the Naval & Military Press Ltd (*www.naval-military-press.com*). Also included is a historical description by Dr Peter Chasseaud, the founder of the Historical Military Mapping Group of the British Cartographic Society, covering the making, printing and use of trench maps; how to understand them and decipher the wartime abbreviations.

Looking at exactly the same piece of ground . . . but in a different century! The transformation is equally unbelievable as this corner of the Flanders battlefield was hotly contested throughout the war and every yard was fought over from October 1914 to September 1918. The church was rebuilt to the original design on the old foundations.

The introduction of vertical cameras transformed the ability to produce photographs from which accurate trench maps could be created. This was first used during the preparations for the Battle of Neuve Chapelle which began on March 10, 1915.

GOOGLE EARTH

Following the First World War, the images on glass negatives were put into storage and all but forgotten. However, Francis Wills, who had served as an observer with the Royal Naval Air Service, decided to use the knowledge he had gained by launching the first commercial aerial photography company. Together with his co-founder, aviation pioneer Claude Graham White, Aerofilms began operations in 1919 from Stag Lane aerodrome at Edgware. In 1921 the company began carrying out vertical photography with Ordnance Survey, one of its main clients, which led in the 1930s to the ability to create and update mapping using aerial photographs.

During the Second World War, the company's staff provided the nucleus for the setting up of the Allied Photographic Interpretation Unit at Medmenham in Buckinghamshire. Aerofilms was acquired by Simmons Mapping (UK) Ltd in 1997 and in 2005 that company was taken over by the Norwegian concern Blom.

That same year the world of aerial photography was turned upside down with the launch of Google Earth on the internet. A small American company, Autometric led by Robert Cowling, had initially created the concept for rendering the entire globe in a project called Edge Whole Earth which had the catch phrase: 'From outer space to in your face'. Keyhole Inc., funded by the Central Intelligence Agency, then created a programme called EarthViewer 3D and this was the company that was acquired by Google in 2004.

Google Earth is created by superimposing imagery obtained from satellites, aerial photography and NASA's Shuttle Radar Topography Mission to provide 3D images. The images are not all taken at the same time but generally are current to within three years. In February 2009, photography dating back to 1940 was added for some locations.

This shot, unfortunately undated, shows the opposing front lines (British on the left and German on the right). At this point no man's land is several hundred yards wide.

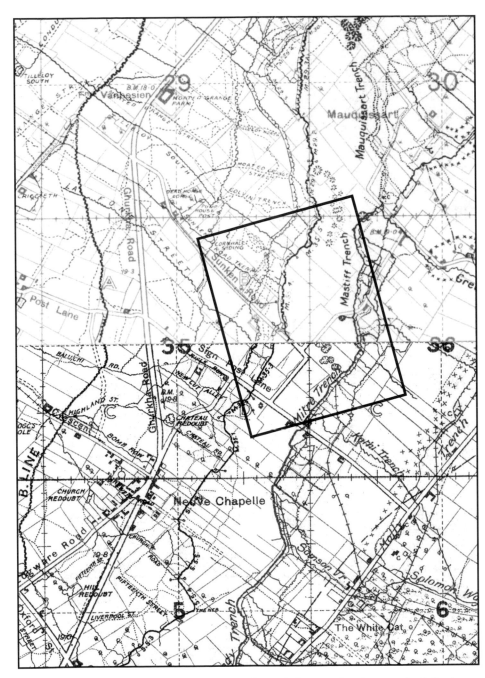

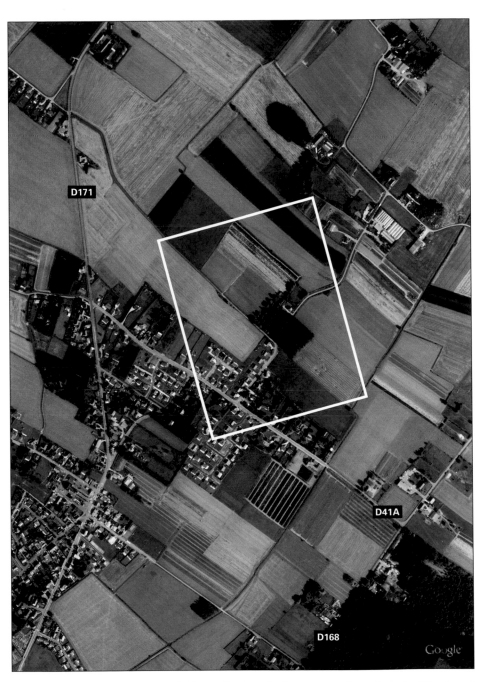

As the 1917 map indicates, the photograph showed the trenches just north of the town. Later, in 1918, the colouring of German trenches was changed from red to blue.

Just like old soldiers, the trench lines of a hundred years ago have faded with almost nothing to show where so many men fought and died.

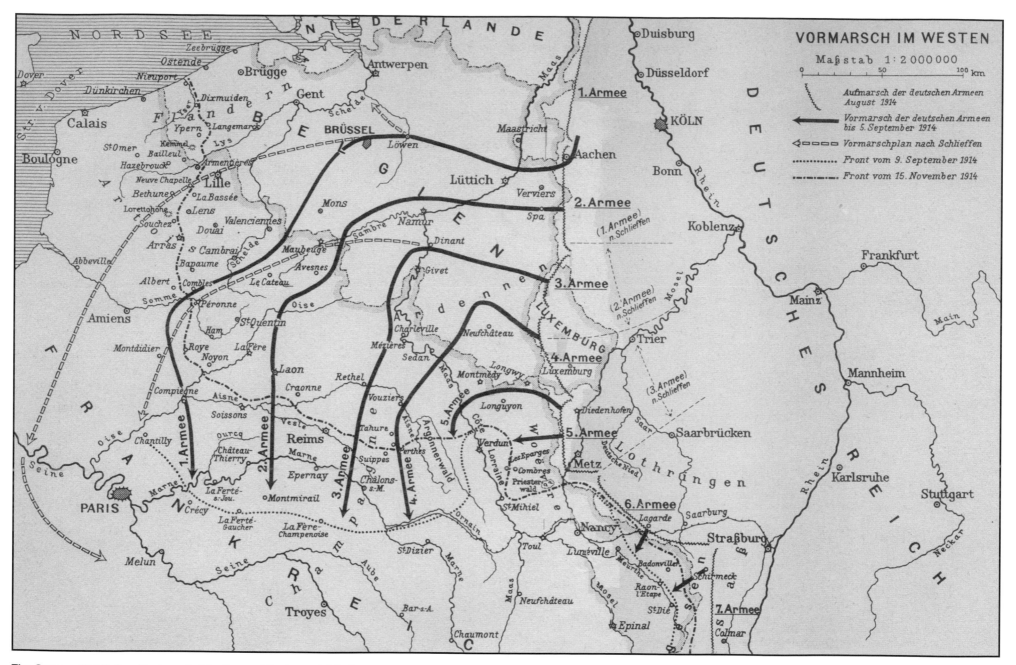

The German 'Schlieffen Plan' created by Count Alfred von Schlieffen was a strategy for a possible future war in Europe. Its purpose was to deliver a quick knock-out blow in the West before turning to face Russia. In modified form the plan was executed by Helmuth von Moltke in 1914 and it very nearly gave Germany a quick victory in the first month of the war. However, a French counter-attack saved Paris (the Battle of the Marne), and the early entry of Russia creating a second front led to stalemate and four years of trench warfare.

Chronology of the Western Front

1914

June 28: Assassination of Archduke Franz Ferdinand of Austria, the heir to the Austro-Hungarian throne, and his wife Duchess Sophie, in Sarajevo. The following month Austria-Hungary ask for German support for a war against Serbia.

July 28: Austria-Hungary declares war on Serbia. Russia mobilises.

August 1: Germany declares war on Russia.

August 2: Germany invades Luxembourg.

August 3: Germany declares war on France and Belgium. The following day Germany invaded Belgium intending to try to outflank the French army. Britain protests against the violation of Belgian neutrality

August 4: The United Kingdom declares war on Germany.

August 4-16: The Germans besiege and then capture the Belgian fortresses at Liège.

August 6: Austria-Hungary declares war on Russia; Serbia declares war on Germany.

August 7: First troops of the British Expeditionary Force (BEF) arrive in France.

August 9: Montenegro declares war on Germany.

August 11: France declares war on Austria-Hungary.

August 12: The United Kingdom declares war on Austria-Hungary.

August 14-28: The Germans obtain early victories against France in Lorraine and the Ardennes.

August 20: The Germans occupy Brussels.

August 22: Austria-Hungary declares war on Belgium.

August 23: Japan declares war on Germany. The first encounter by the BEF in the Battle of Mons.

August 25: The Germans capture the French fortress at Namur.

August 25: Japan declares war on Austria-Hungary.

August 26-27: Battle of Le Cateau. The Allies are forced to retreat.

August 29-30: Battle at Saint Quentin and Guise leads to an Allied retreat.

September 5-12: First Battle of the Marne when the German advance on Paris is halted.

September 12-15: Battle of the Aisne — the 'Race to the Channel' begins.

September 22-26: First Battle of Picardy.

September 22-25: First Battle of Albert.

September 27-October 10: First Battle of Artois.

September 28-October 10: The Germans capture Antwerp.

October 1-4: First Battle of Arras.

October 10-November 2: Battle of La Bassée.

October 12-November 2: First Battle of Messines.

October 13-November 2: Battle of Armentières.

October 16-November 10: Battle of the Yser. French and Belgian forces secure the Belgian coastline.

October 19-November 22: First Battle of Ypres — the Germans are prevented from reaching Calais and Dunkirk.

October 21-24: The First Battle of Langemarck.

October 29-31: Battle of Gheluvelt.

November 11-22: Battle of Nonneboschen.

1915

March 10-13: Battle of Neuve Chapelle. The beginning of static trench warfare but the British offensive is halted after an initial success.

April 17-22: Battle of Hill 60 – first operation to plant mines underneath the German positions.

April 22-May 25: Second Battle of Ypres at which the Germans first use chlorine gas.

May 9-June 18: Second Battle of Artois.

September 25-October 15: Third Battle of Artois.

September 25-October 8: Battle of Loos, at which the British first use gas.

1916

January 27: Conscription introduced in the United Kingdom by the Military Service Act.

February 21-December 18: Battle of Verdun.

July 1-November 18: Battle of the Somme.

July 1-13: Battle of Albert.

July 1: Gommecourt Salient attack.

July 14-17: Battle of Bazentin.

July 19-20: Battle of Fromelles.

July 20-25: Attacks at High Wood.

July 15-September 3: Battle for Delville Wood.

July 23-September 3: Battle of Pozières.

August 18-September 5: Battle of Guillemont.

August 30: Paul von Hindenburg appointed German Chief of General Staff.

September 9: Battle at Ginchy.

September 15-22: Battle of Flers-Courcelette. The first use of tanks.

September 25-28: Battle of Morval.

September 26-28: Battle of Thiepval.

October 1-18: Battle for Le Transloy.

October 1-November 11: Battle of the Ancre Heights.

October 24: The French recapture Fort Douaumont at Verdun.

November 13-15: Battle of the Ancre marks the closing phase of the Battle of the Somme.

November 18: The Battle of the Somme ends.

1917

February 23-April 5: The Germans withdraw to the Hindenburg Line.

April 6: The United States of America declares war on Germany.

April 9-May 16: Battle of Arras. The British attack the heavily fortified German line in a series of operations.

April 9-14: First Battle of the Scarpe.

April 9-12: Battle of Vimy Ridge.

April 10-11: First Battle of Bullecourt.

April 15: Battle of Lagnicourt.

April 23-24: Second Battle of the Scarpe.

April 28-29: Battle of Arleux.

May 3-4: Third Battle of Scarpe.

May 3-17: Second Battle of Bullecourt

June 7-8: The British recapture Messines Ridge.

June 25: First American troops land in France.

July 31: Third Battle of Ypres begins.

July 31-August 2: Battle of Pilckem Ridge.

August 16-18: Second Battle of Langemarck.

September 16-18: Battle of the Menin Road.

September 26-October 3: Battle of Polygon Wood.

October 4: Battle of Broodseinde.

October 9: Battle of Poelkapelle.

October 12: First Battle for Passchendaele.

October 26-November 10: Second Battle of Passchendaele.

November 20-December 7: Battle of Cambrai.

November 5: The Allies agree to establish a Supreme War Council at Versailles.

November 10: The end of the Third Battle of Ypres.

1918

March 21-April 5: First phase of the German 'Spring Offensive' (Operation Michael).

March 21-23: Battle of St Quentin.

March 24-25: First Battle of Bapaume.

March 25: First Battle of Noyon.

March 26-27: Battle of Rosières.

March 26: French Marshal Ferdinand Foch is appointed Supreme Commander of all Allied forces.

March 28: Battle at Arras.

April 1: Royal Air Force founded by combining the Royal Flying Corps and the Royal Naval Air Service.

April 4: The second phase of the 'Spring Offensive' (Operation Georgette begins).

April 9-11: Battle of Estaires.

April 10-11: Battle of Messines.

April 12-15: Battle of Hazebrouck.

April 13-15: Battle of Bailleul.

April 17-19: Battle for Kemmel Ridge.

April 18: Battle for Béthune.

April 25-26: Further Battle for Kemmel.

April 29: Battle of Scherpenberg.

May 27-June 2: Third Battle of the Aisne (Operation Blücher-Yorck — the third phase of the 'Spring Offensive').

May 28: First US attack in the Battle at Cantigny.

June 6-July 1: Battle of Belleau Wood.

June 9-13: Final phase of the 'Spring Offensive' (Operation Gneiseau).

July 4: Battle of Le Hamel.

July 15-August 5: Second Battle of the Marne and last German offensive on the Western Front.

August 8-11: Allied offensive begins for Amiens — the first phase of the 'Hundred Days' offensive.

August 21: Second Battle of the Somme begins.

September 12: Battle of Havrincourt.

September 12-16: Battle of St Mihiel.

September 18-October 10: Battle of the Hindenburg Line - the Allies break through the German lines.

September 26-November 11: Allied Meuse-Argonne Offensive, the final phase of the First World War.

September 29-October 2: Battle of the St Quentin Canal.

September 30: Bulgaria signs an armistice with the Allies.

October 3-5: Second Battle of Cambrai.

October 14-19: Battle of Courtrai.

November 1: Battle at Valenciennes.

November 4: Battle of the Sambre.

November 9: Kaiser William II abdicates - republic proclaimed in Germany.

November 10: Kaiser Charles I of Austria-Hungary abdicates.

November 11: At 6 a.m. Germany signs the Armistice at Compiègne. Fighting ends at 11 a.m.

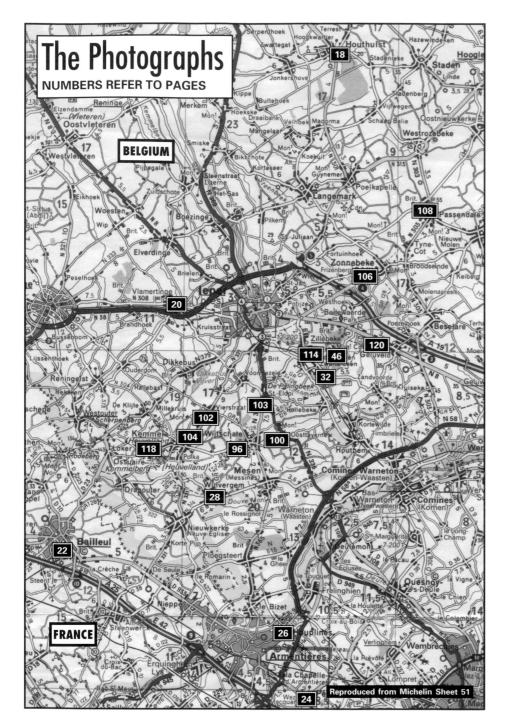

The Photographs
NUMBERS REFER TO PAGES

BELGIUM

FRANCE

Reproduced from Michelin Sheet 51

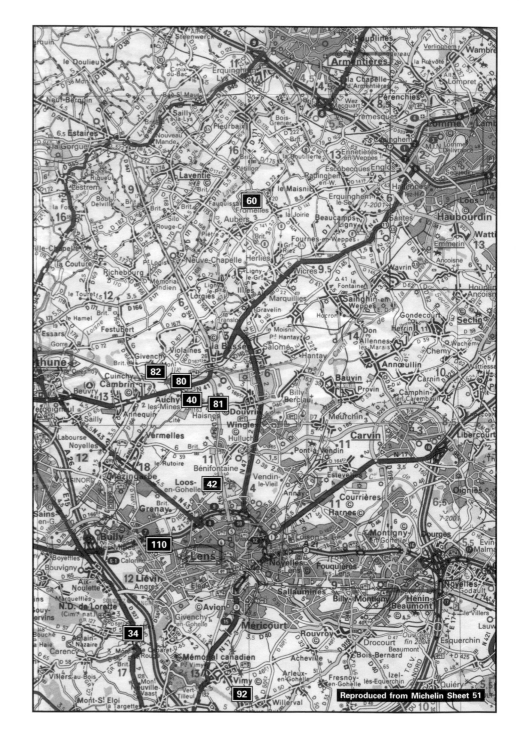

Reproduced from Michelin Sheet 51

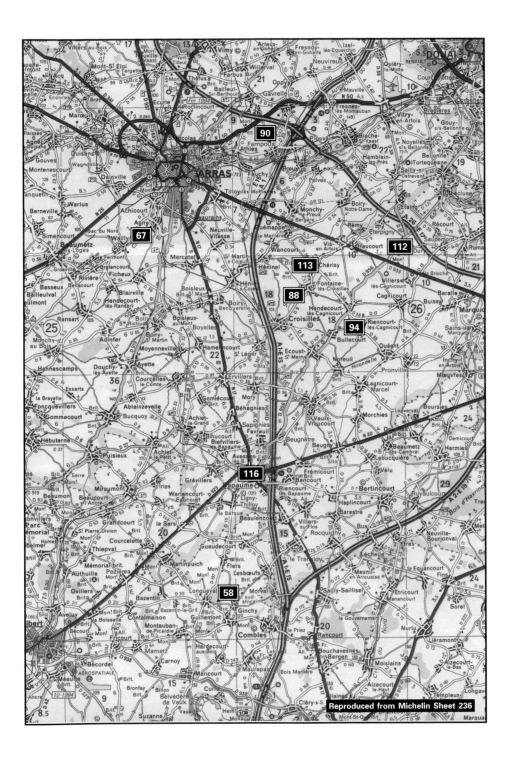

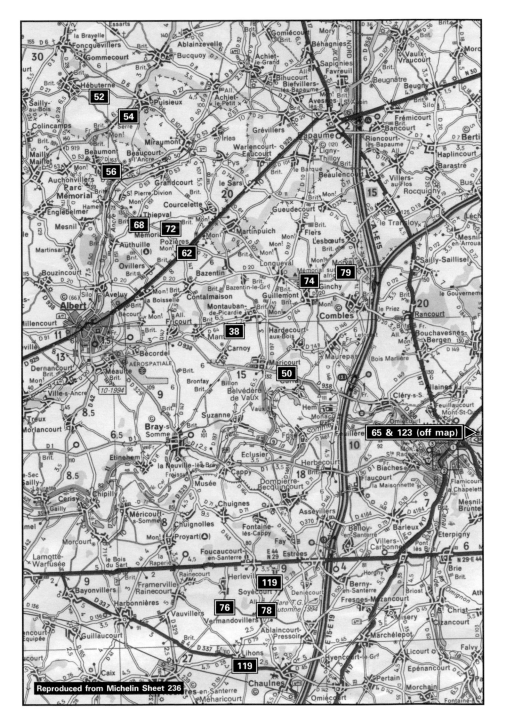

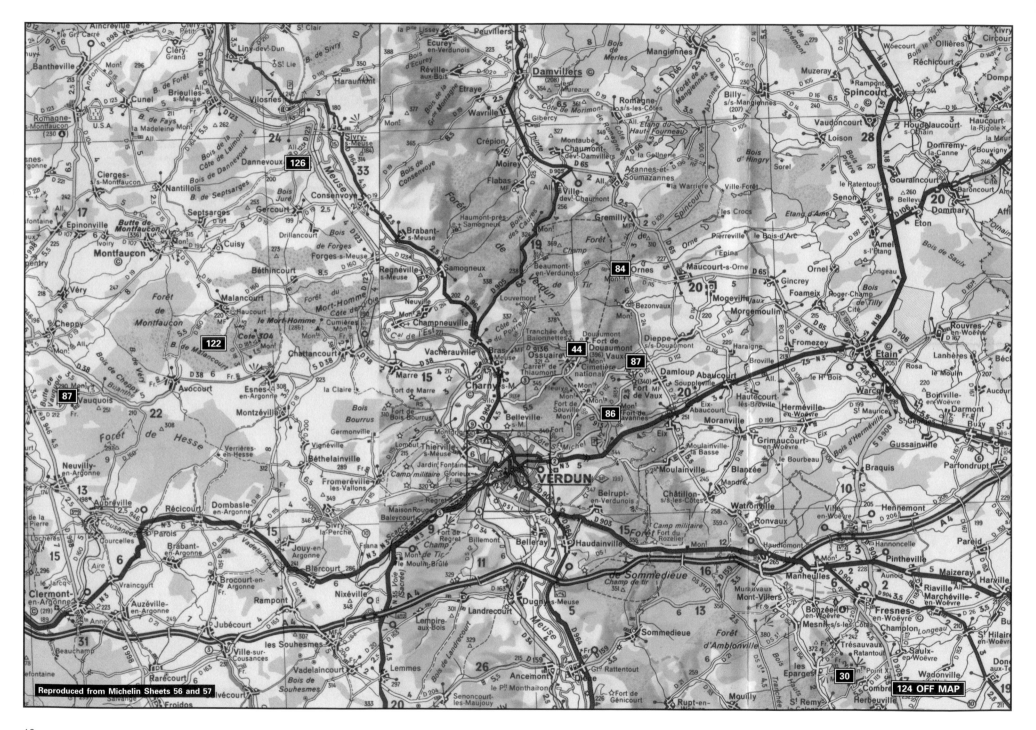

Tens of thousands of young French lives were lost in the battlefields around Verdun. Over a thousand miles to the east Hector Dinning, a soldier serving with the 6th Company of the Australian Service Corps, set down his thoughts as the ill-fated campaign on Gallipoli came to its end. He wrote that 'the day is far off when splending mausolea will be raised over the heroic dead. And one foresees the time when steamers will bear pilgrims come to do honour at the resting places of friends and kindred, and to move over the charred battlegrounds'. Surely a fine epitaph to the sacrifice of all soldiers everywhere. At Verdun, the cemetery and ossuary at Douaumont stand testimony to those Frenchmen who left home, never to return.

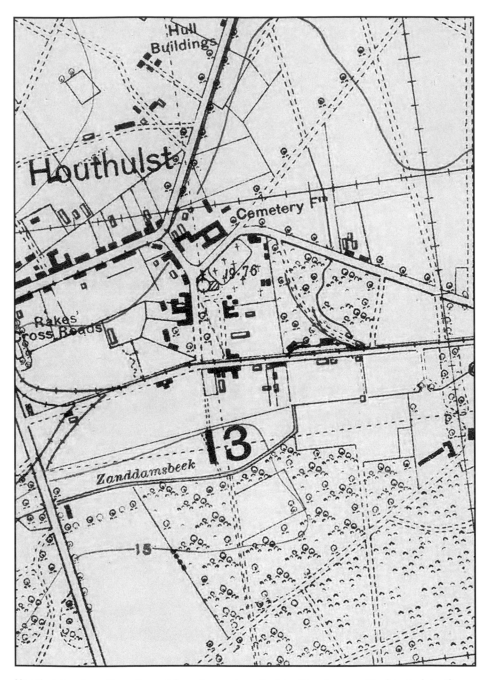

Houthulst, where the adjacent forest was described by Napoleon as the key to Low Countries, fell to the Germans on October 21, 1914 after a gallant defeat by the Belgian Army

with the support of French cavalry. The Germans fortified the whole of the forest and the Belgians were not able to recapture their territory until the end of September 1918.

TO DIKSMUIDE

N301

TO POELKAPELLE

Google

19

Just to the west of Ypres lies Vlamertinge which was in German hands between October 7-10, 1914. The British Army established a network of camps around the town, taking over a cemetery in April 1915 which had been begun by the French. This was used until June 1917 when a second cemetery was begun. By 1918 only the tower of the church remained standing.

The faded 1918 photogaph shows the eastern edge of the town which, as the Google Earth cover shows, has greatly expanded. The railway in the picture running from Poperinge, which lies a few miles to the west, Courtrai (Kortrijk) in the east was a vital means of getting supplies up to the front.

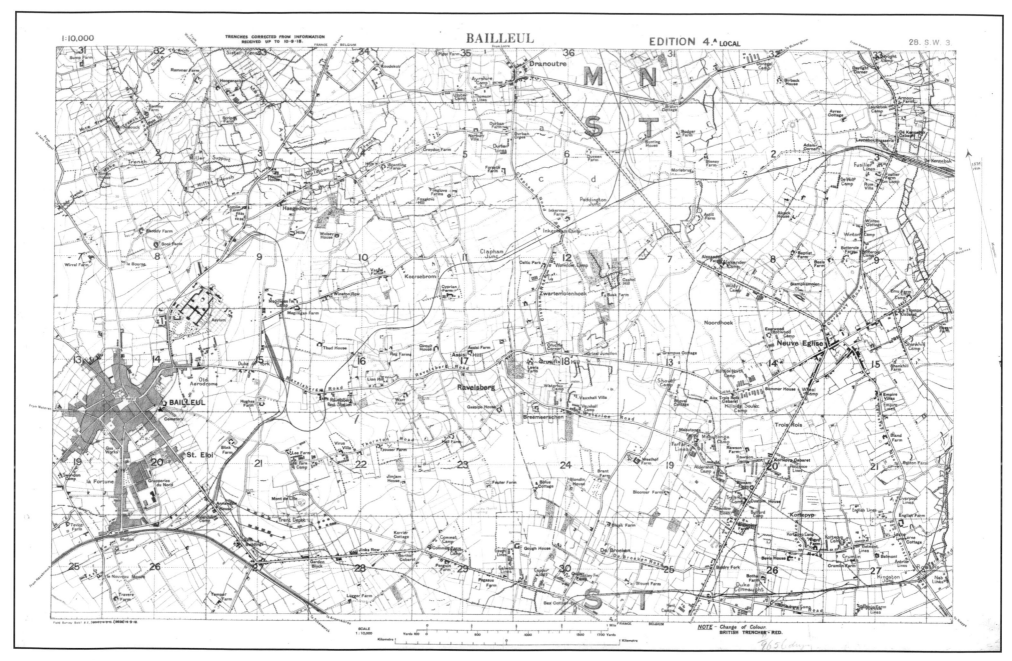

Moving south across the frontier to France, for most of the war Bailleul was spared the fate of the towns nearer the front line. It was a popular rest area and provided a welcome respite from life in the trenches and as a forward military base it had hospital facilities for the wounded. However, in July 1917, German shelling began and by April 1918 when it fell, it was a shattered ruin. Bailleul remained in German hands until August 30 when the British 25th Division regained possession. On this 1918 map the British trenches are now in red.

One of those camps is illustrated here. Alexander Camp lies on the join of Map Squares T 7 and 8 in the trench map reproduced on the opposite page. The road which runs diagonally across the photo is the N322 to Neuve-Eglise just out of the photograph.

It changed hands several times in April 1918 until, after severe fighting, the 25th Division was finally driven out. It was not until September 2 that it was back in Allied hands, thanks to the efforts of the 36th (Ulster) Division.

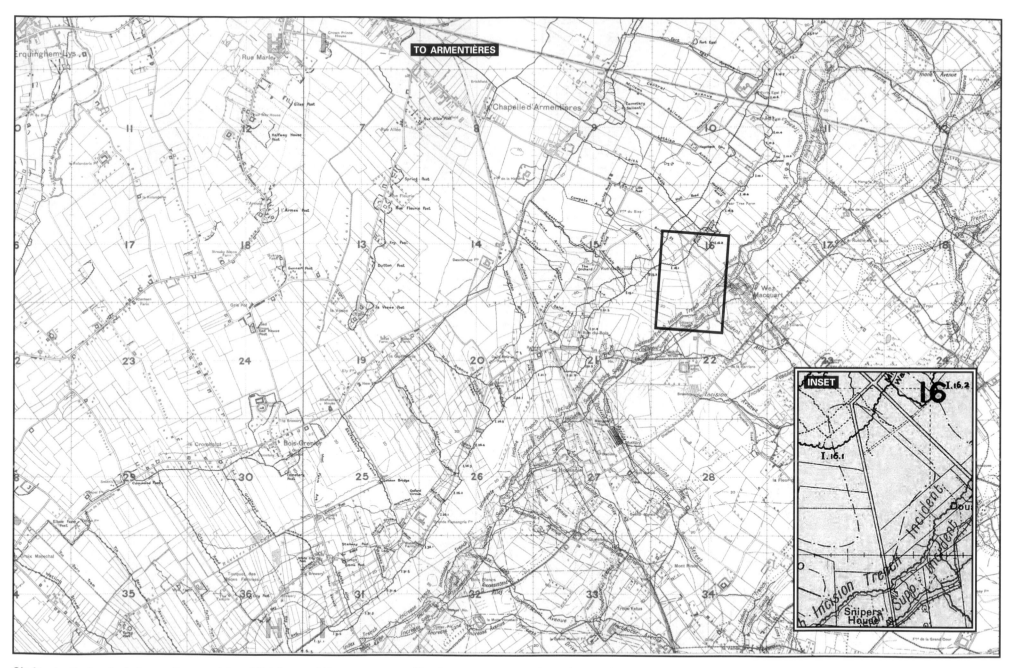

Obviously, the border between the countries of Belgium and France meant nothing in war, yet the first large town of Armentières did . . . certainly in the bawdy song — a favourite with the Old Contemptibles — supposedly about a certain Mademoiselle de Bar le Duc.

Apart from a short period in 1914, Armentières lay just behind the Allied line which appears in detail on this map in the traditional British colour of blue as this is a September 1917 map. Note the village of Wez Macquart in Map Square 16.

TO ARMENTIÈRES

D933

Wez Macquart lying right behind the German front line has virtually ceased to exist. No man's land between the British and German lines at this point is just over 200 yards.

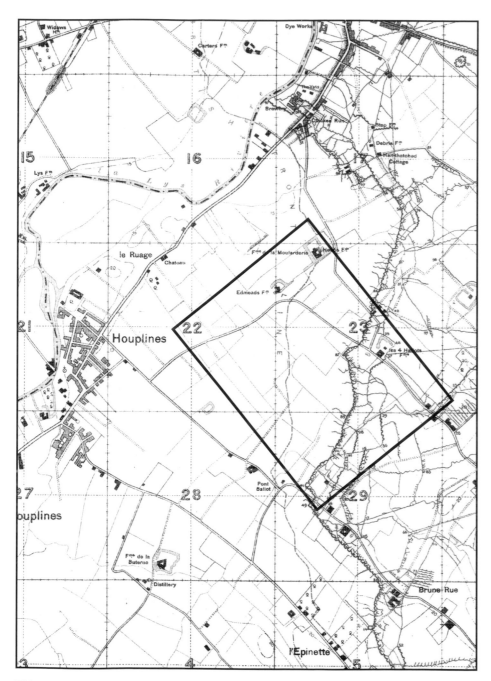

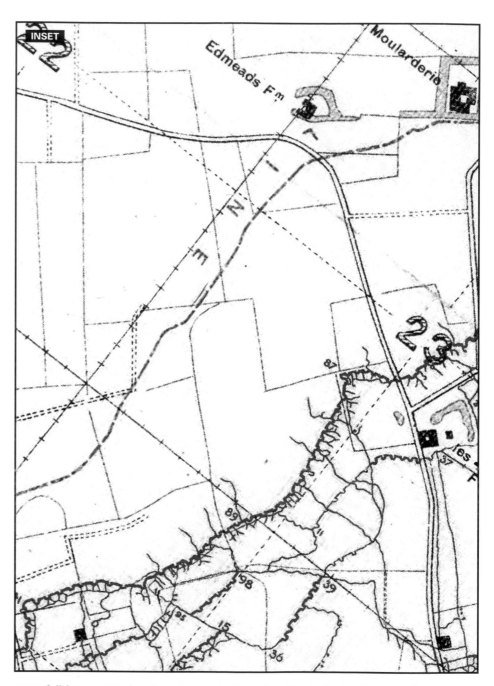

This map covering Houplines, then a village but now a suburb of Armentières, is a good example of the early period when the British trenches were not shown in detail in case the maps fell into enemy hands so just a single broken line indicated the front. It must have been almost like fighting with one hand tied behind one's back!

The photograph was taken in July 1915 by No. 4 Squadron which had been one of the first units to experiment with aerial photography. They went to France in August 1914.

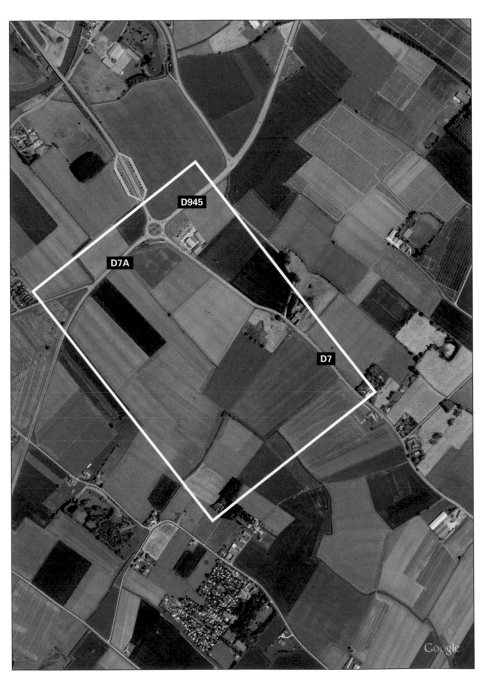

Today the D945 slices across the battlefield, the D7 having the rather poignant name of Chemin de l'Aventure.

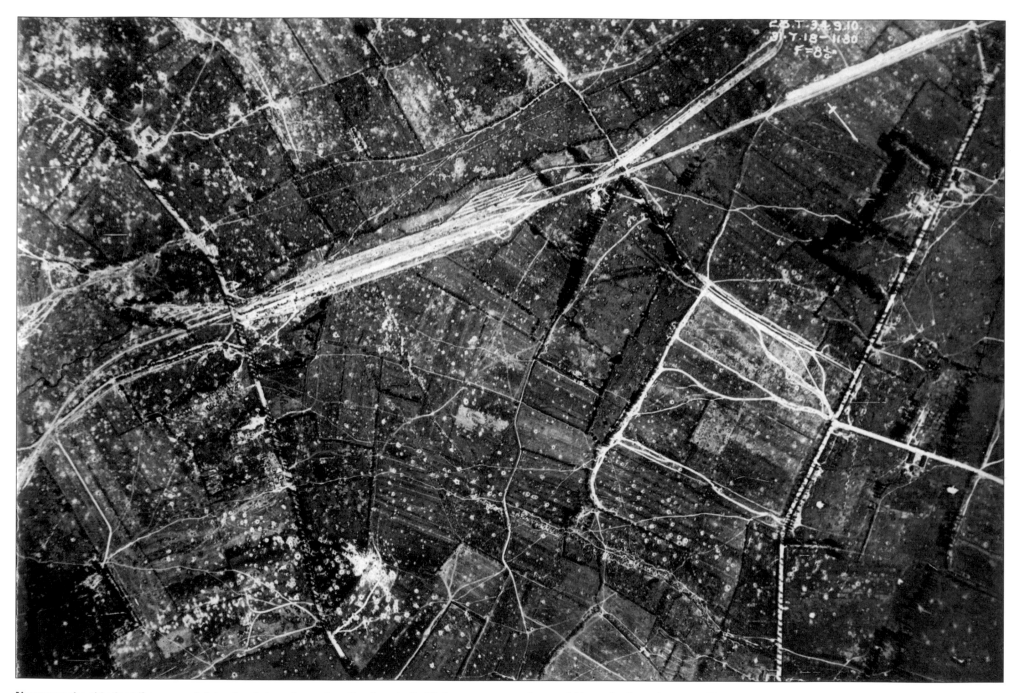

Never was the old adage 'from swords into ploughshares' more true than here in the Wulvergem area north-east of Alexander Camp (page 23). The railway siding can be seen in Map Square T 3 on page 22.

WULVERGEM-LINDENHOEK CEMETERY

In an attempt to capture Wulvergem the Germans used a gas attack in 1916 although it still did not fall into their hands until 1918. The cemetery alongside the N314 was first called Wulvergem Dressing Station Cemetery and was begun in December 1914. It contained 162 graves at the time of the Armistice. It was then decided to enlarge it and rebury casualties from other scattered burial grounds: Auckland Cemetery at Messines (12 New Zealanders); the nearby Cornwall Cemetery (21 soldiers); Frenchman's Farm (30 soldiers); Neuve-Eglise North (20 soldiers), and Neuve-Eglise Railway Siding Cemetery (14 soldiers). Today over a thousand Commonwealth servicemen lie in Wulvergem-Lindenhoek Cemetery of whom 352 are unidentified.

The Crête des Eparges — a dominating ridge of high ground ten kilometres south-east of Verdun, was occupied by the Germans in September 1914. It was fought over tenaciously by the French, the 12ème Division d'Infanterie gaining the position on April 5, 1915 after mines were detonated beneath the German line. Attack and counter-attack followed and 16 French divisions and four American divisions fought for this piece of ground until the end came in September 1918 but the cost was high with casualties running into thousands.

Vestiges of the trenches are still visible, overshadowed by the line of craters left from the detonation of the mines.

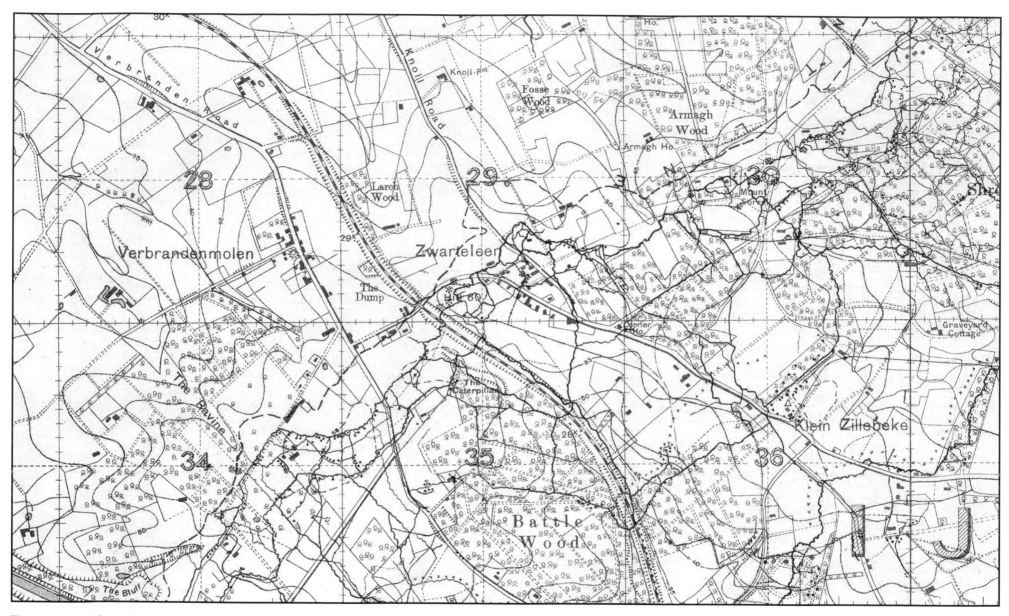

The high ground from which Hill 60 got its name was created from the spoil excavated from the cutting created during the construction of the Ypres-Comines railway. After the Germans captured the hill in December 1914, a plan was formulated to undermine and blow up the enemy fortifications on the crest. Five chambers were dug under the hill and packed full with explosives which were detonated early on April 17, 1915. Shelling and counter-shelling followed with the British units vehemently holding their positions throughout several attacks preceded by gas but by May 7 the Germans had regained possession of Hill 60.

The British had suffered over 3,000 casualties in trying to retain and recapture Hill 60. Now further excavating took place in order to position two huge mines underneath the German line. These were set off on June 7, 1917 together with a chain of mines which had been laid to begin the battle for Messines (see page 102). After the mines exploded, Hill 60 was captured with few casualties, the Germans having lost several hundred men. This map extract is from August 1916 with the British positions still not marked other than the blue dotted line to include the front. Hill 60 is in Map Square 29 just below Zwarteleen.

The craters left by the two large mines — one on Hill 60 itself and the other on what was called the Caterpillar position on the far side of the railway line — remain to be seen today.

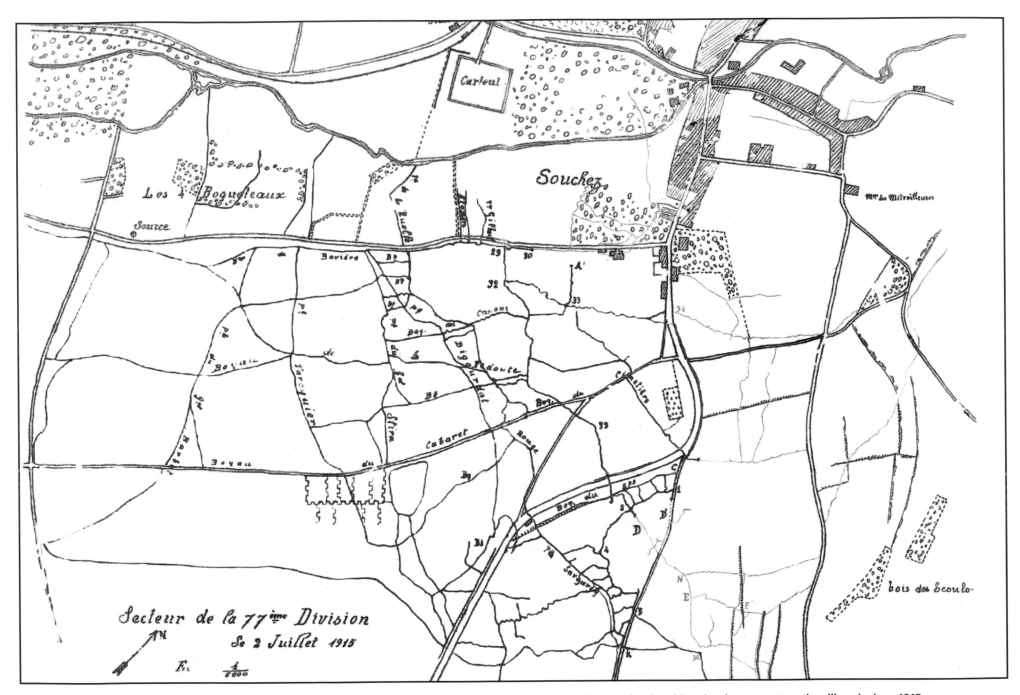

This French plan shows the trench layout at Souchez, just west of Givenchy-en-Gohelle, where the French 77th Division fought a bitter battle to recapture the village in June 1915.

SOUCHEZ

D58

77th DIVISION MEMORIAL

A26

MATCHES PHOTOS, PAGES 36-37

D937

CABARET ROUGE CEMETERY

MATCHES TRENCH MAP PAGE 34

Three months later the French finally succeeded in capturing Souchez but in March 1916 this area was transferred to the British although by then the village was in ruins. The memorial to the 77th Division stands beside Rue Carnot (the D937). The Commonwealth Cabaret Rouge Cemetery south of the town which has now greatly expanded, contains 7,655 graves of which 4,471 bear the simple inscription 'Known unto God'. And it was from this cemetery that the remains of an unknown Canadian soldier were exhumed in 2000 to be flown across the Atlantic to be laid to rest in the tomb of the Unknown Soldier at the National War Memorial in Ottawa.

The progression of the battlefield. Unfortunately undated, these two French aerial photographs cover the area outlined on the Google Earth photo on the previous page.

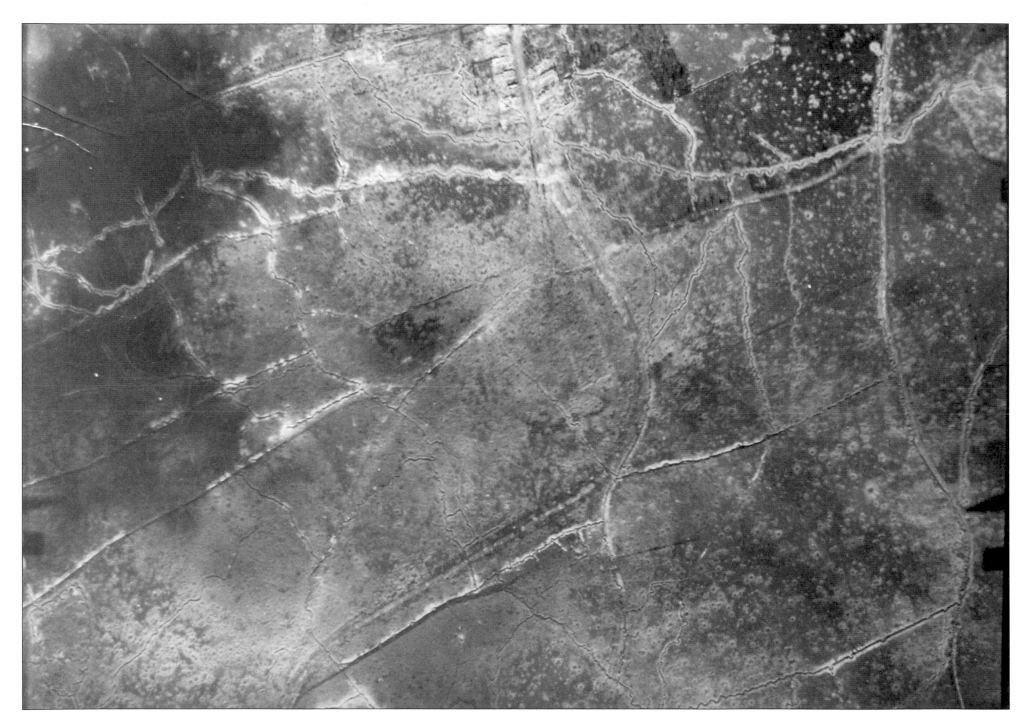

37

The introduction of poison gas during the First World War brought a new horror to the battlefield. The first instance of it being used was on April 22, 1915 when the German Army released chlorine north of Ypres. It occurred again on three subsequent occasions during the Second Battle of Ypres. Although the British expressed their horror at such 'a cowardly form of warfare', at the same time it was realised that the same weapon would have to be employed.

The British retaliated on September 25 that year in the Battle of Loos but it proved a disaster as the wind turned and German shelling struck full cylinders, releasing gas amongst British troops. This picture shows a British attack in the Somme sector in June 1916, the gas being released on either side of the road between Carnoy (bottom right) and Montauban (top left). The latter town was successfully captured on July 1. Photograph taken looking south-east.

MONTAUBAN-DE-PICARDIE

MARICOURT

D64

CARNOY

A combination of chlorine and phosgene was released by the Germans in December and mustard gas in July 1917. A nurse, Vera Brittain, described the symptons: 'Great mustard-coloured blisters, blind eyes, all sticky and stuck together, always fighting for breath, with voices a mere whisper, saying that their throats are closing and they know they will choke.'

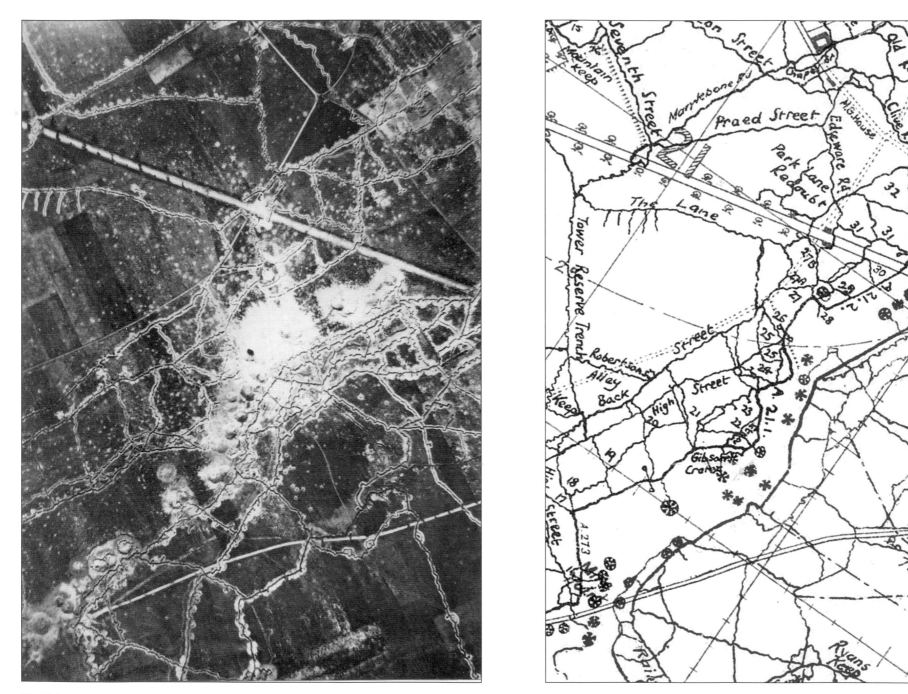

The Hohenzollern Redoubt, a formidable German strong point, was taken by the 9th (Scottish) Division in the Battle of the Loos fought in 1915 from September 25 to October 19, although later lost.

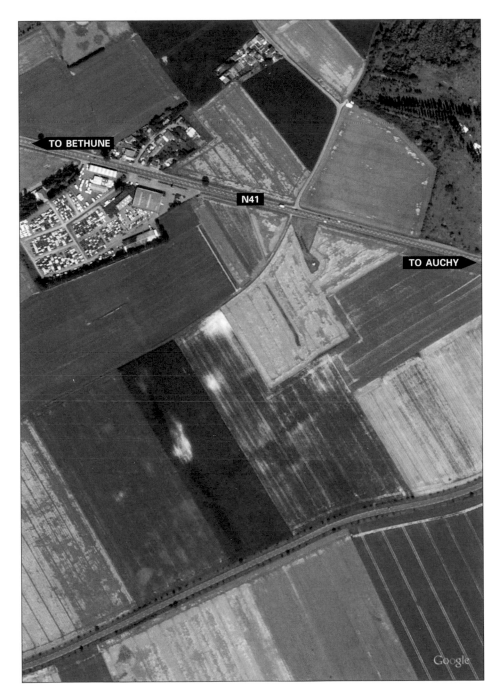

Depending on the season, the former earthworks west of Auchy-les-Mines still show through the soil. This photo *(left)* was taken in December 2004 and *(right)* in June 2006.

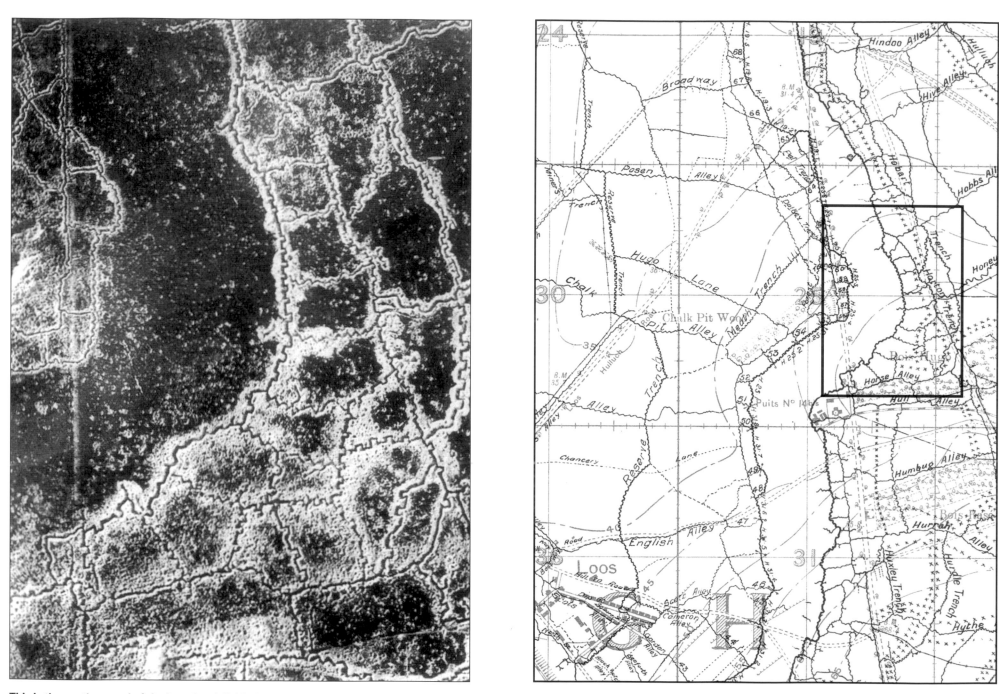

This is the southern end of the Loos battlefield, the town itself lying out of the photograph to the south-west. Note Chalk Pit Wood in Map Square 30.

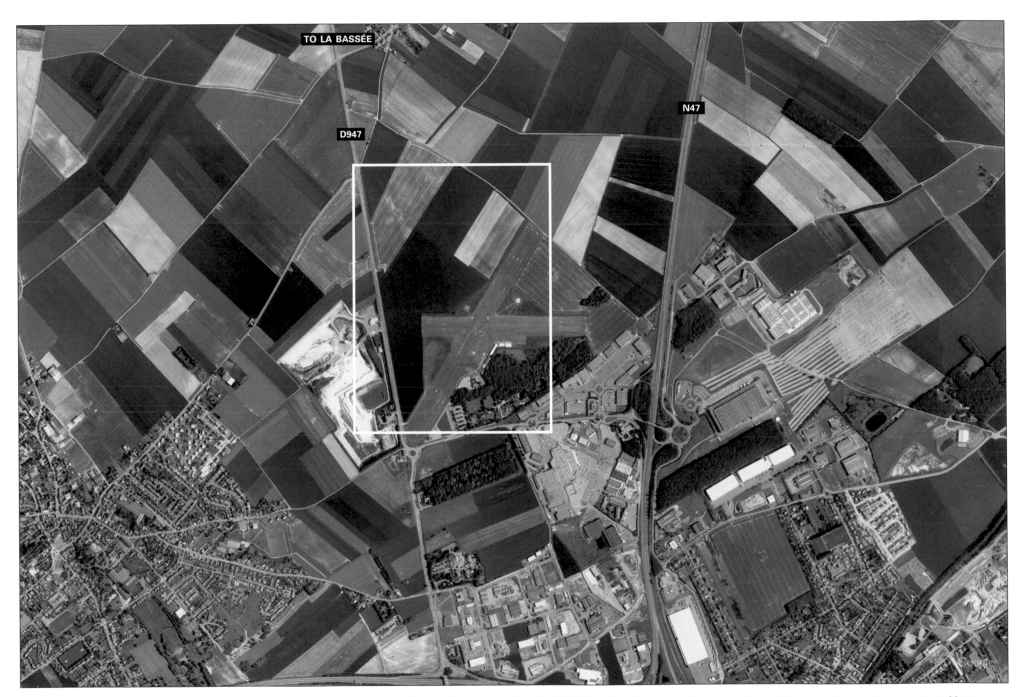

The road running north-south leading to La Basée passes Loos-en-Gohelle airfield on the eastern side. Chalk Pit Wood has lived up to its name as the white scar indicates the current workings.

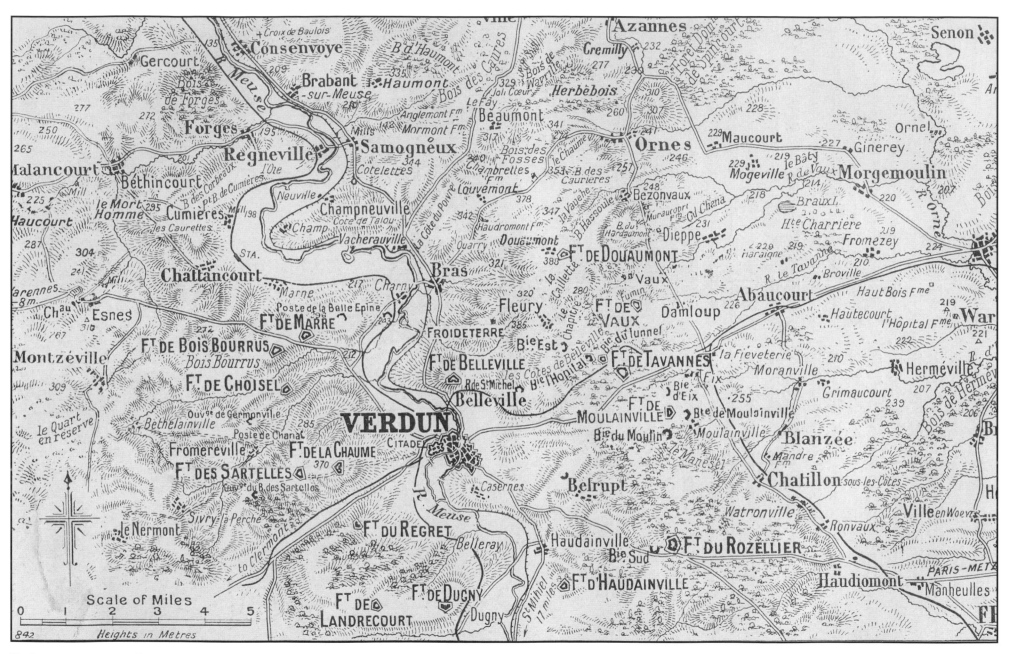

Verdun in north-eastern France on the River Meuse has always held an important place in European history having been fought over since the Middle Ages. It came into French ownership in 1648 but was besieged by the Prussians in 1792 and occupied by them from 1870-73. As a result a ring of forts was constructed to prevent the same thing happening again and by 1914 it was considered the 'great advanced citadel of France'. However, the following year the forts were robbed of their heavy armament which was desperately needed elsewhere on the French line leaving the garrisons — and the city — very vulnerable. In Churchill's words: 'Verdun was the anvil upon which French manhood was hammered to death'.

The first to fall was also the most important: Fort de Douamont, which was captured after a battle lasting just five days. That was in February 1916 — this photo being taken on April 23 — yet the Germans suffered greviously just two weeks later when the ammunition magazine exploded killing over 600 and wounding another 1,800 of their men.

Next came Fort de Vaux just to the south. The German operation against this fortress began on June 1, 1916 when intensive artillery fire and flame-thrower attacks subjected the 250-strong garrison to such a battering that, with no chance of relief and no fresh water, after six days they were forced to surrender.

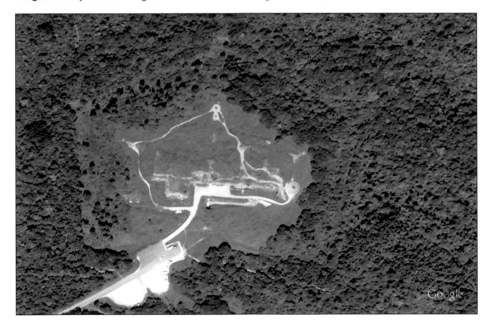

The battle of Mount Sorrel — or the battle of Hill 62 as it was also known — was fought between three divisions of the British Second Army and three from the German Fourth Army. This particular battle also marked the first occasion in the war that Canadian forces engaged in an offensive operation, an enterprise which successfully regained the vital high ground essential for the defence of Ypres. This trench map gives an overview of the battlefield two miles south-east of the city as it appeared in January 1917. In the centre lies Sanctuary Wood and the high ground of Hills 61 and 62 with Mount Sorrel just to the south. Although the high ground between Hooge and Zwarteleen was less than 50 feet above the surrounding countryside, it was vital that it be held to prevent the Germans being able to place artillery there which could then threaten Ypres. Back in 1914, the wood lived up to its name as Brigadier-General Edward Bulfin used it as a place of sanctuary for his 2nd Infantry Bigade but by early 1915 it was very close to the front line. In May that year the Germans were in possession of the eastern end of the wood while the British and French occupied the western part. In June 1916 the Canadian Corps was defending the high ground and was already planning its offensive to advance eastwards when the Germans launched their own long-prepared assault in an attempt to divert British resources from the impending operation on the Somme. The Battle of Mount Sorrel began on June 2 taking the Canadians by surprise, well over three-quarters of the men becoming casualties including two commanding officers. Then, at 1 p.m., the Germans detonated four mines heralding an attack by infantry which advanced up to 1,200 yards to capture Mount Sorrel and Hill 61. A Canadian counter-attack the following day proved abortive with heavy losses but a second, larger assault was planned to follow a ten-hour bombardment of the German positions on June 12. The next morning, more heavy shelling followed before the troops went forward under the cover of smoke. In this, the Canadians were almost completely successful in regaining their original trenches.

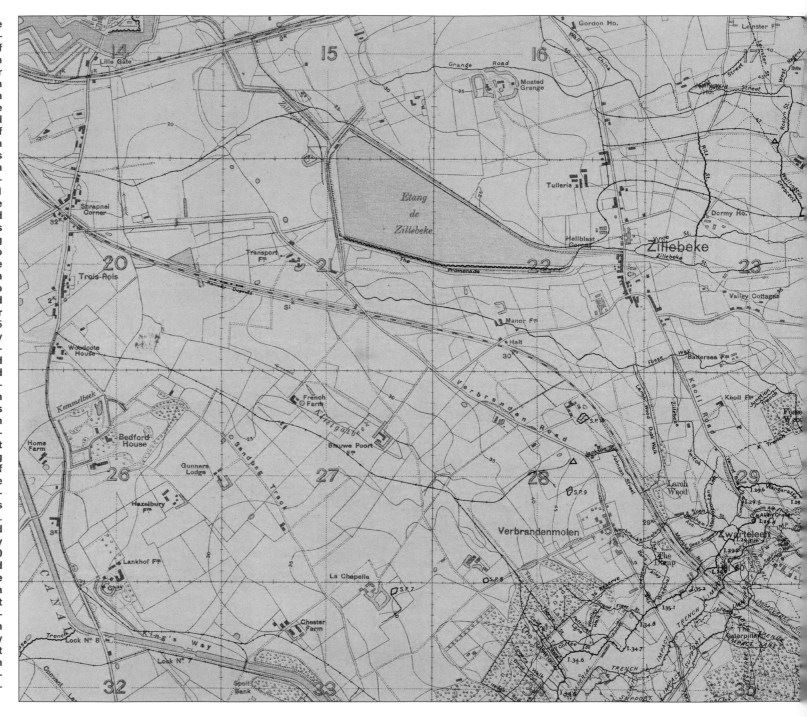

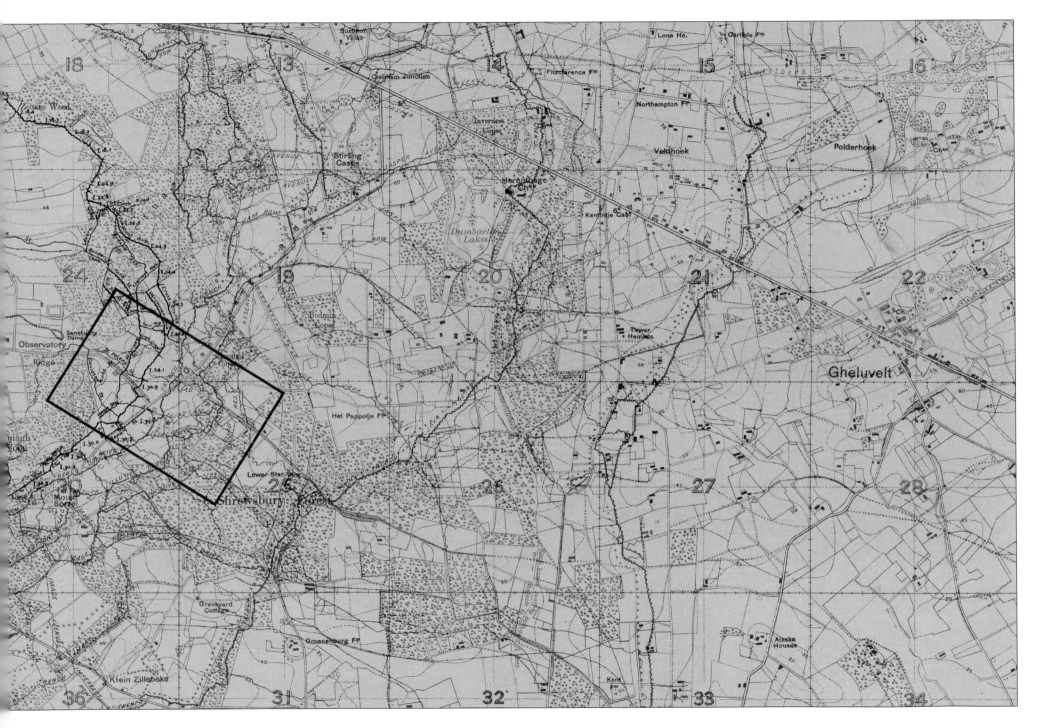

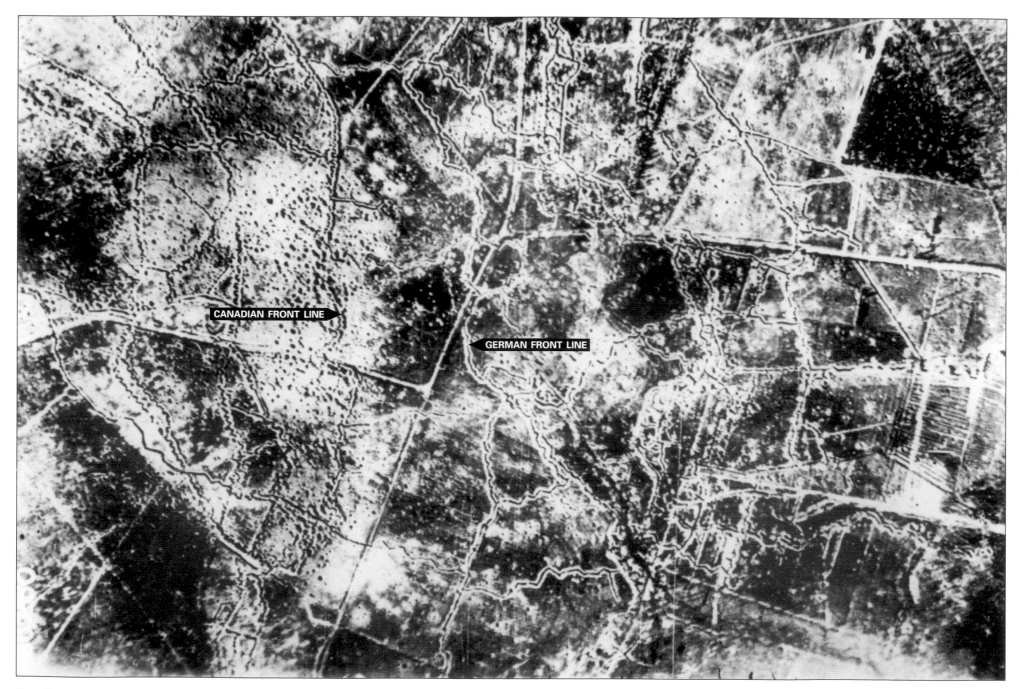

CANADIAN FRONT LINE

GERMAN FRONT LINE

Zooming into the war-torn battlefield at the southern end of Sanctuary Wood (as shown on the inset on previous page) where the front lines were barely 100 yards apart.

ZILLEBEKE

N8

When the Canadian Battlefield Monument Commission was established after the war, it selected eight locations for the placing of memorials and it was originally envisaged that the main Canadian National Memorial should be placed on Hill 62 but this was later voted down in favour of it being sited at Vimy (see pages 92-93).

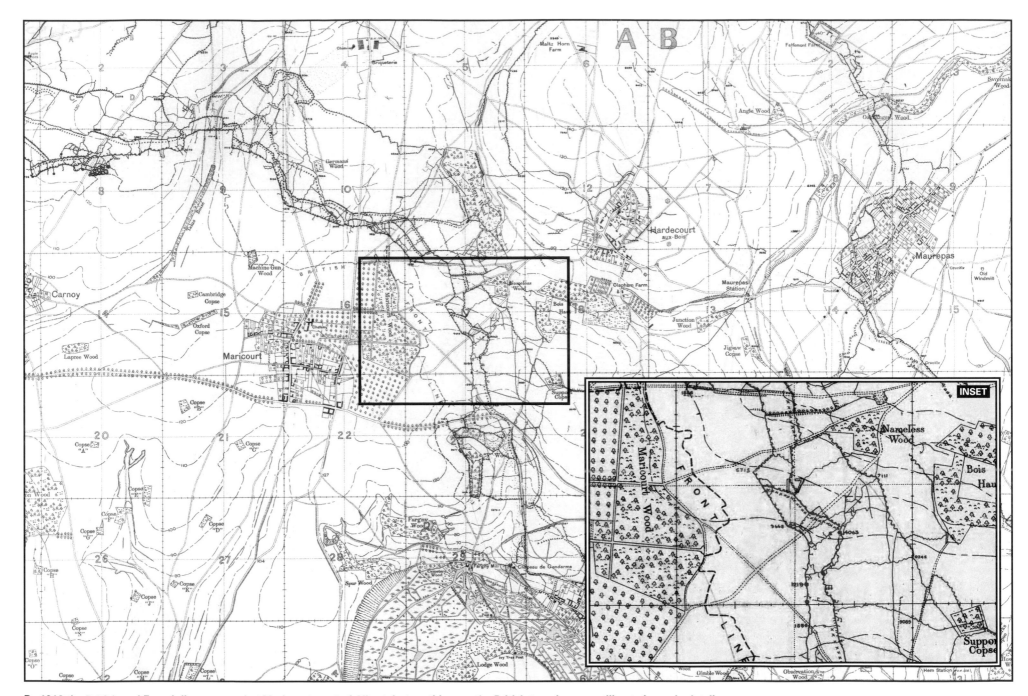

By 1916 the British and French lines merged at Maricourt, east of Albert, but on this map the British trenches are still not shown in detail.

INSET

The large Google Earth view shows exactly the same area as shown on the trench map. Inset is the front line section east of Maricourt Wood as appears in the inset photograph.

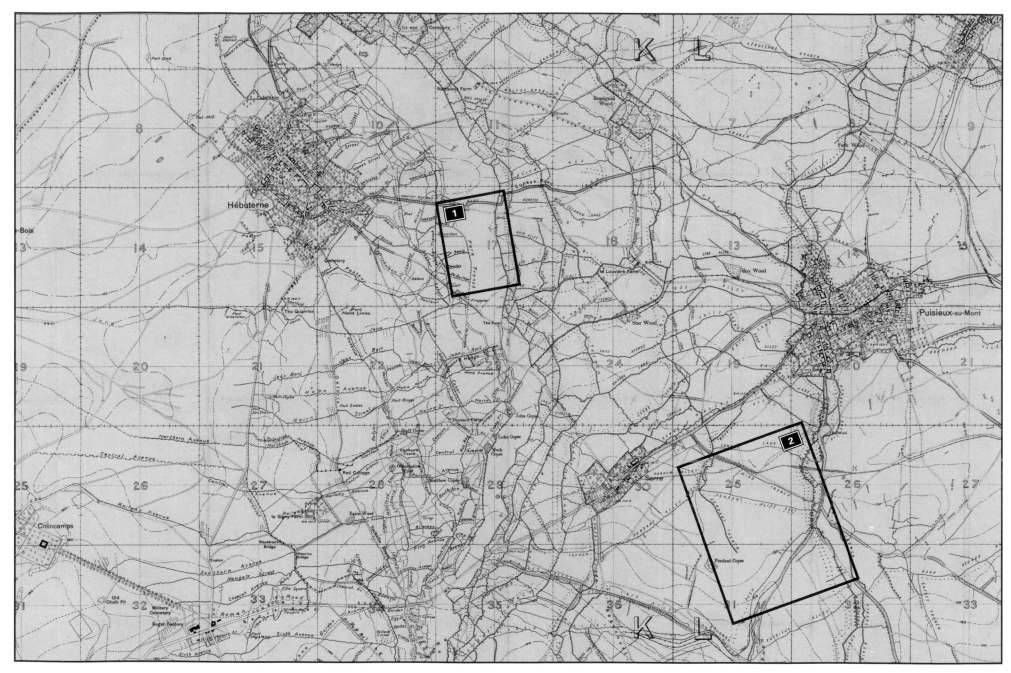

We are now approaching the area where the Battle of the Somme took place in 1916. The British trench system on this map now being included in detail as at November 26, 1916.

Over the next pages we illustrate two different aspects: no man's land east of Hébuterne [1] and the German second line of defence near Serre [2]

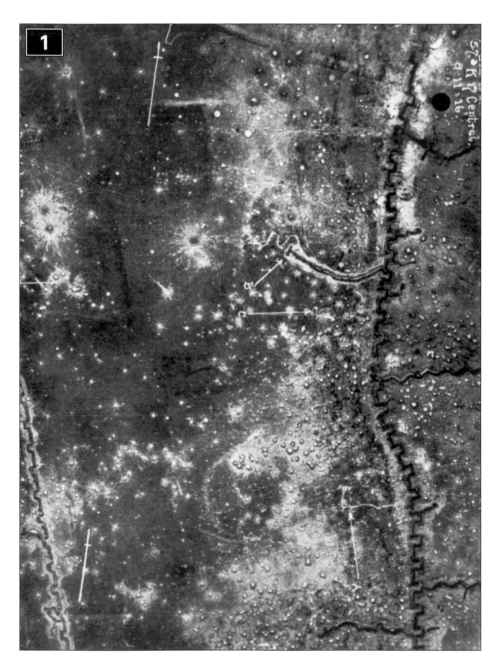

This photo was taken after heavy rain in November 1916 — the same month the map was updated. Clever photo-interpretation has identified 'A' as a track made by a listening patrol to a shell-hole in front of the wire; 'B' is a waterlogged sap with tracks made by a patrol walking along its edge, and 'C' a dry shell-hole most probably being occupied by a listening post.

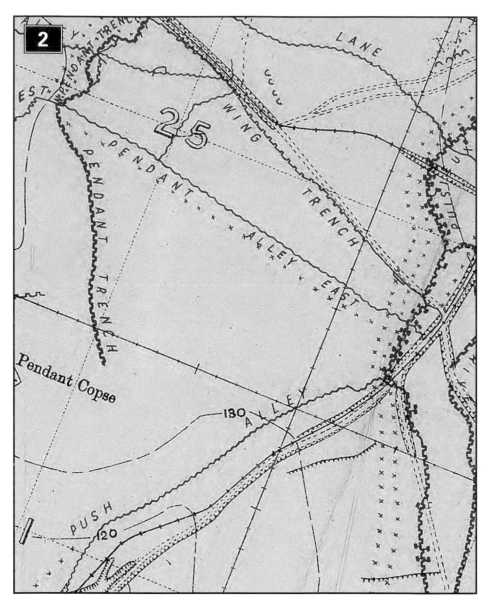

Serre experienced very severe fighting and several cemeteries and memorials now stand as silent witnesses to the dead of Britain, France and Germany. Many of the French fell during an attack in June 1915 and the British on July 1, 1916. The interpretation included with this photo showing the German second line of defence in October that year, is unfortunately rather feint on this print. 'AA' to 'B' marks a communication trench being converted into a fire trench, the white spots being piles of chalk which have been excavated for dugouts along its length. 'CC', 'DD' and 'EE' are belts of wire, the white lines on either side of 'DD' and 'EE' being the tracks left by the wiring party. 'LL' is a narrow-gauge railway and 'MM' is a road.

The British losses at Serre were from several of the so-called 'Pals battalions' which had been recruited from specific towns and cities, and the nickname was coined as many of those who enlisted were friends. They hoped they would remain together through their service life . . . and thus whole streets suffered with their deaths. At 7.20 a.m. on July 1, the men of the 31st Division left their trenches and began to cross no man's land which was barely 200 yards at that point but most were mown down by machine-gun fire before they were half-way across. They came from Sheffield, Leeds, Bradford and Barnsley. Although one company of the Accrington Pals did reach Serre, none of them returned.

SERRE

D919

2

Google

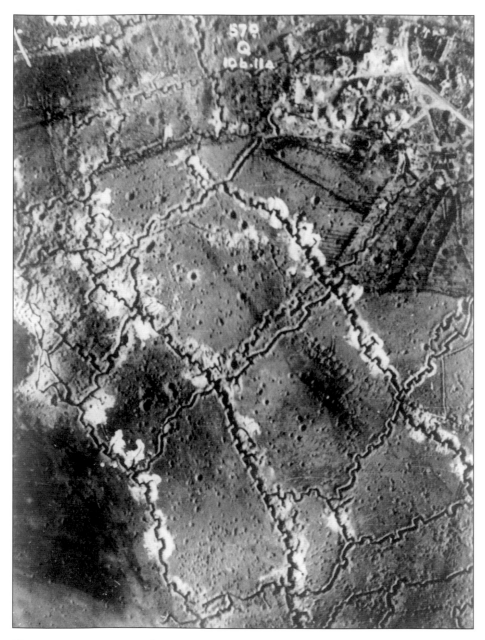

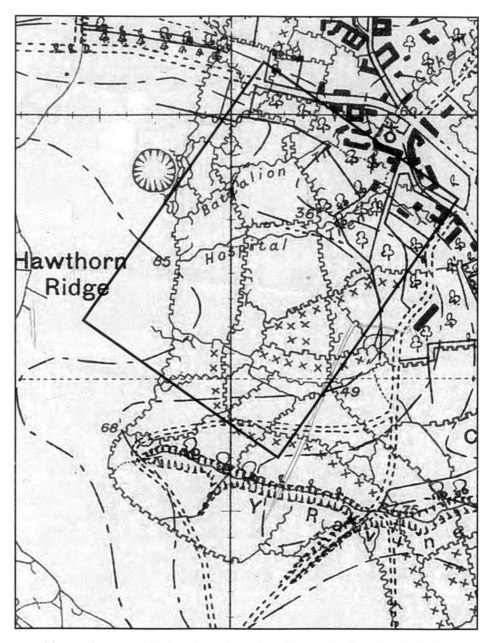

The assault on Beaumont-Hamel on July 1, 1916 was heralded by the premature explosion of a mine which had been laid beneath the Germans' Hawthorn Redoubt. This led to the British guns ceasing their pre-attack shelling to enable the troops to capture the huge crater; consequently nothing was achieved for the cost of 13,000 men killed. Of those, 684 men of the 1st Battalion of the Royal Newfoundland Regiment became

casualties — the second highest loss of any battalion on the first day of the Somme. Unfortunately, Hawthorne Ridge Crater — created by 18 tons of explosive — is just out of the photograph. Later in November 1916 a second mine of 13 tons was blown under the first crater when the British resumed the attack when Beaumont-Hamel was finally taken by the 51st (Highland) Division.

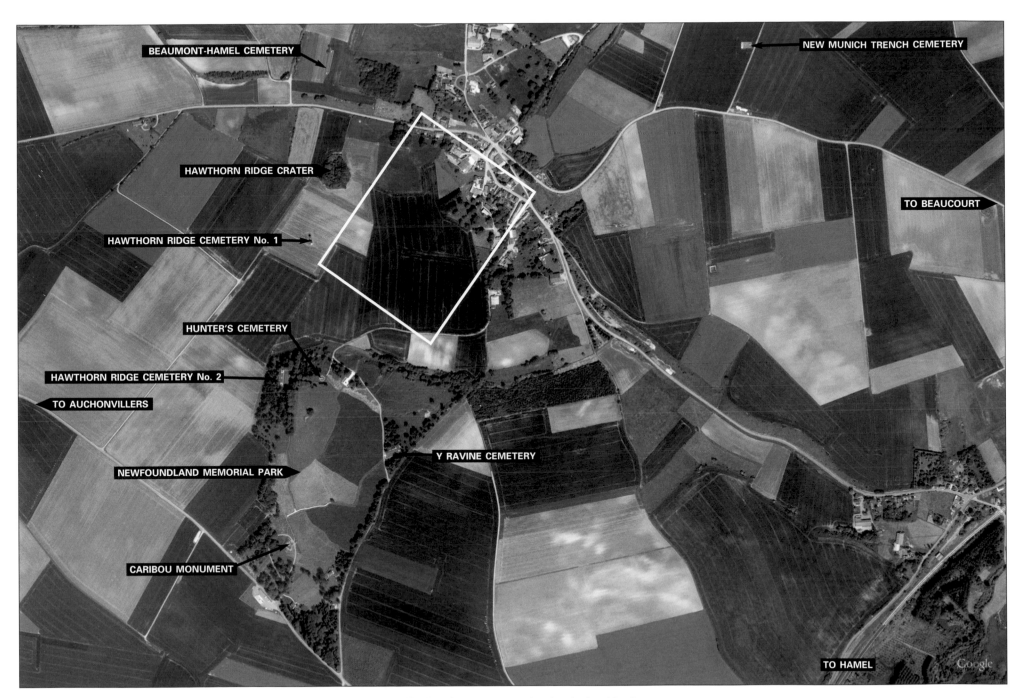

BEAUMONT-HAMEL CEMETERY

NEW MUNICH TRENCH CEMETERY

HAWTHORN RIDGE CRATER

TO BEAUCOURT

HAWTHORN RIDGE CEMETERY No. 1

HUNTER'S CEMETERY

HAWTHORN RIDGE CEMETERY No. 2

TO AUCHONVILLERS

Y RAVINE CEMETERY

NEWFOUNDLAND MEMORIAL PARK

CARIBOU MONUMENT

TO HAMEL

Part of the battlefield at Beaumont-Hamel has been preserved as a Memorial Park and many cemeteries dot the local landscape.

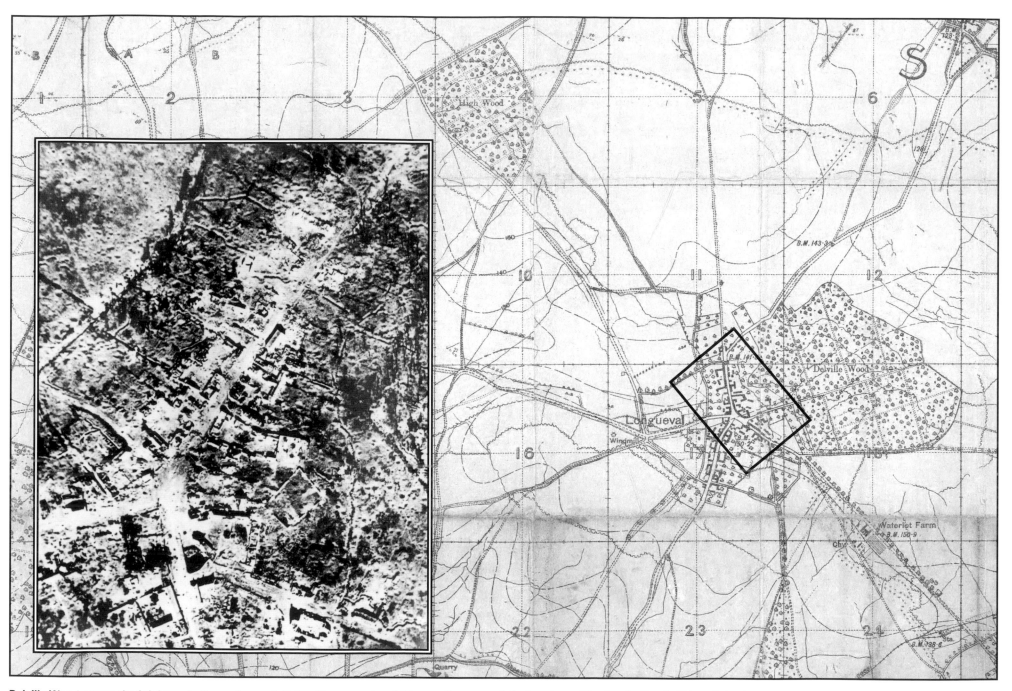

Delville Wood encroached right up to the eastern outskirts of Longueval and this was the scene of the baptism of fire for the South African Brigade in July 1916.

MEMORIAL

DELVILLE WOOD CEMETERY

The battle for possession of the wood began on July 15 and in spite of heavy German artillery fire, within two days the brigade had taken nearly all the wood although the troops that were left were withdrawn on the evening of July 20. The 2nd Division finally cleared the shattered wood on July 28. Today over 5,500 dead lie in Delville Wood Cemetery of whom 3,500 are unidentified. Facing the cemetery is the South African Memorial and the associated museum.

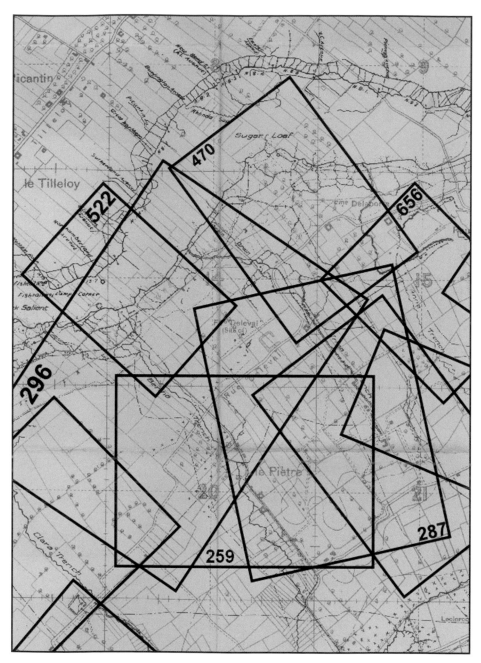

To give one an idea of the scope of aerial reconnaissance photography on the Western Front, this is the coverage of just one small section of the line at Fromelles during the preparations for an attack by the British and Australians (from the blue trenches) in July 1916.

In what has been described as the worst day in the country's entire history, the Australian 5th Division lost over 5,500 casualties in a matter of a few hours while attempting to capture the 'Sugarloaf' position on July 19, 1916. This is Print No. 470.

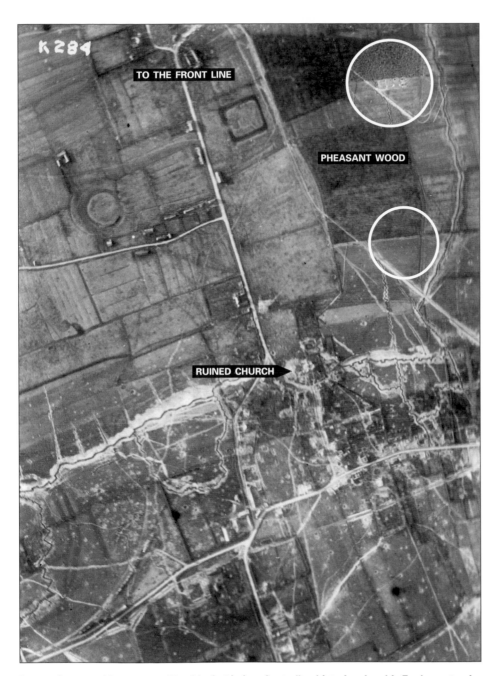

TO THE FRONT LINE

PHEASANT WOOD

RUINED CHURCH

It was photographic coverage like this that led an Australian historian, Lambis Englezos, to pin-point the mass graves used by the Germans to bury the dead. This photo, taken on April 25, 1916, shows the village of Fromelles occupied by the Germans and the road leading to the front.

A photograph taken on August 1 — just two weeks after the battle — revealed a line of pits just south of the wood (circled inset). When these pits were excavated in 2009, the remains of 250 men were discovered, many of whom could still be identified (see *After the Battle* No. 150).

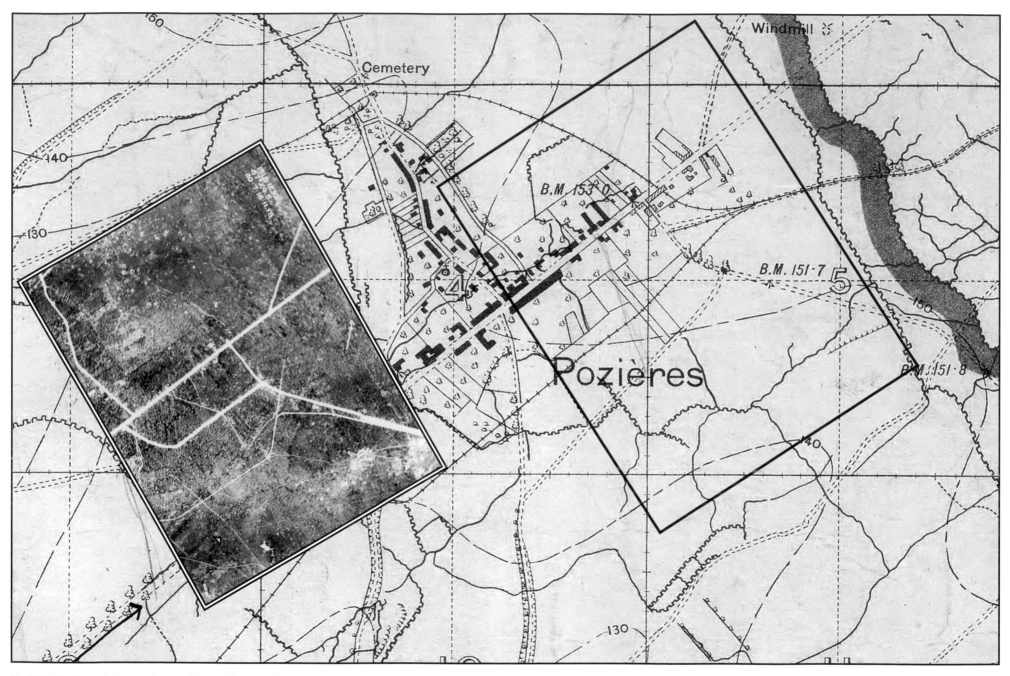

By 1916 Pozières, lying on the road from Albert to Bapaume, had virtually ceased to exist. The ruins were captured by the 1st Australian Division and 48th (South Midland) Division in July that year but were lost to the big German offensive in March 1918. It was finally back in Allied hands in August.

TO BAPAUME

D929

TANK CORPS MEMORIAL

1st AUSTRALIAN DIVISION MEMORIAL

D147

POZIÈRES MEMORIAL AND CEMETERY

TO ALBERT

The Pozières Memorial to the Missing records the names of over 14,000 soldiers who have no known grave. Another 2,756 men are buried in the cemetery of whom over half are unknown.

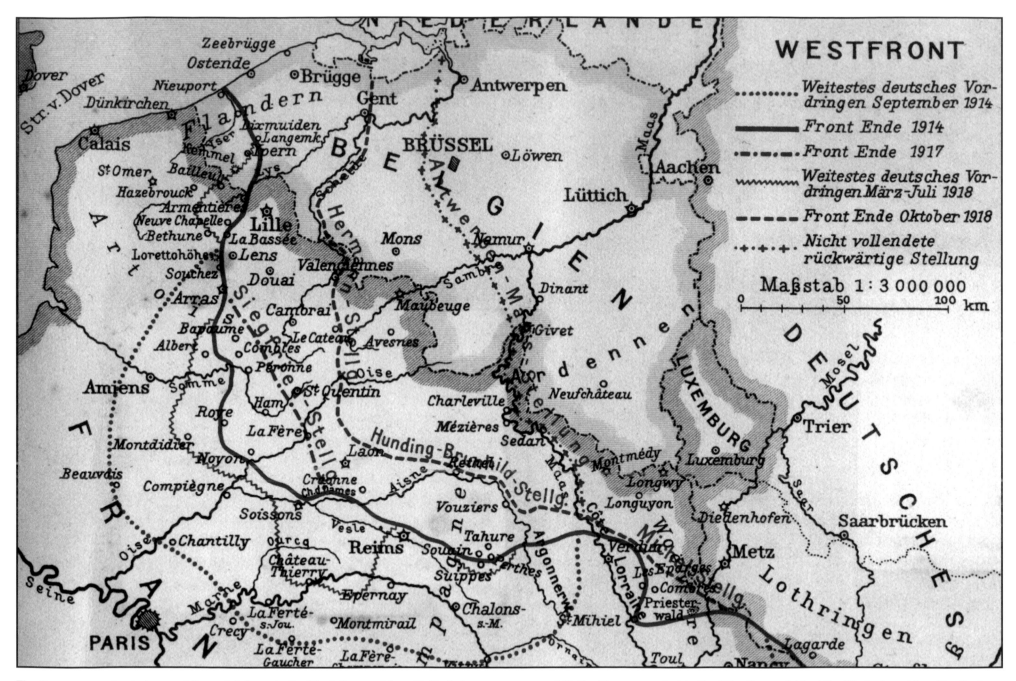

WESTFRONT

- ·········· *Weitestes deutsches Vordringen September 1914*
- —————— *Front Ende 1914*
- —·—·—·— *Front Ende 1917*
- ∿∿∿∿∿∿ *Weitestes deutsches Vordringen März-Juli 1918*
- — — — — *Front Ende Oktober 1918*
- ·—+·—+·— *Nicht vollendete rückwärtige Stellung*

Maßstab 1 : 3 000 000

0   50   100 km

The Germans constructed several lines of defence in the West, the most formidable being the Siegfried-Stellung named after the dragon-slayer in Richard Wagner's operas *Siegfried* and *Gotterdämmerung,* but to the Allies it was dubbed the Hindenburg Line after Paul von Hindenburg who was appointed as Chief of the General Staff in August 1916.

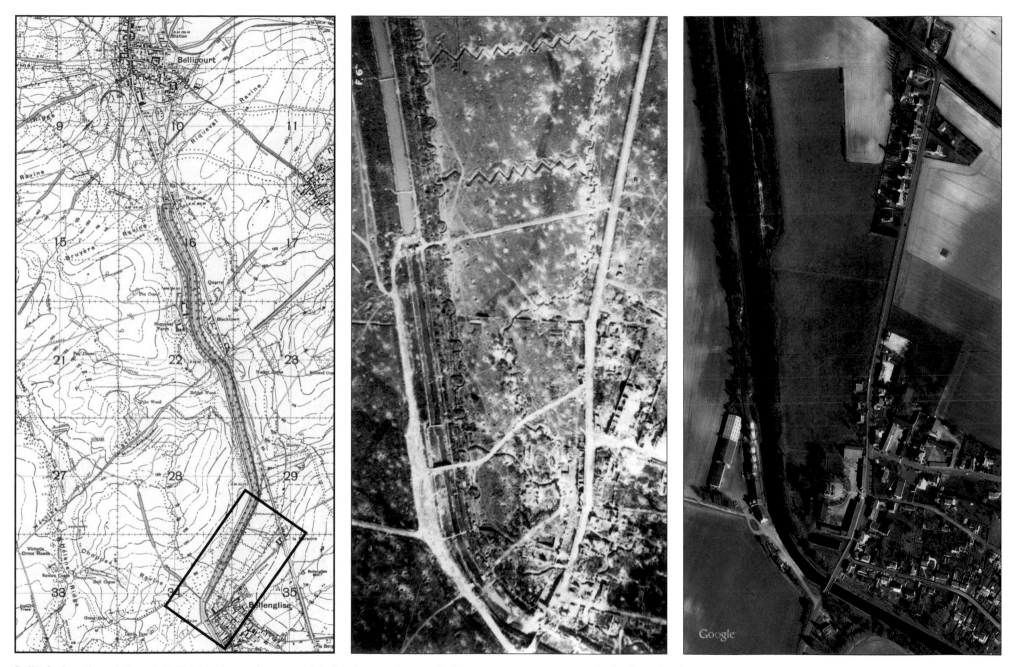

Built during the winter of 1916-17 to be an impenetrable barrier running south from Arras, within the line buildings, roads, bridges and railways were destroyed to create a deep barren zone protected by bands of wire entanglements and elaborate trench systems. At St Quentin the canal was an additional obstacle defended by fortified machine-gun positions although just south of Bellicourt it disappeared in a tunnel over three miles in length. (See also page 123.)

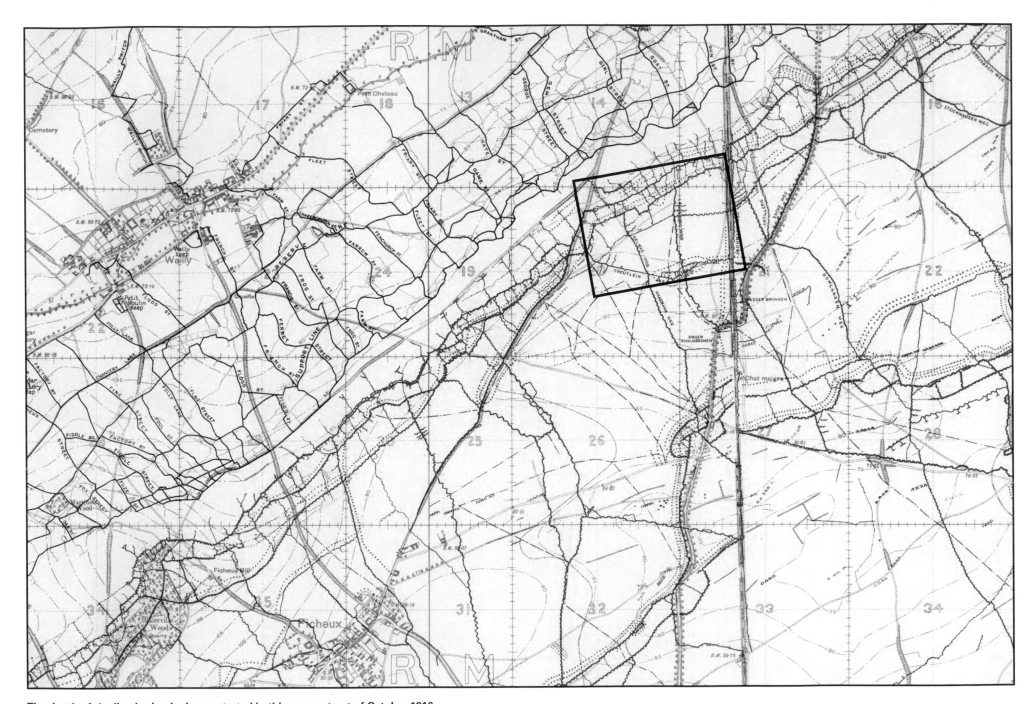

The depth of the line is clearly demonstrated in this map extract of October 1916.

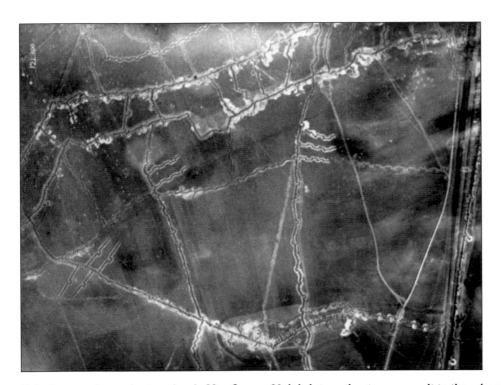

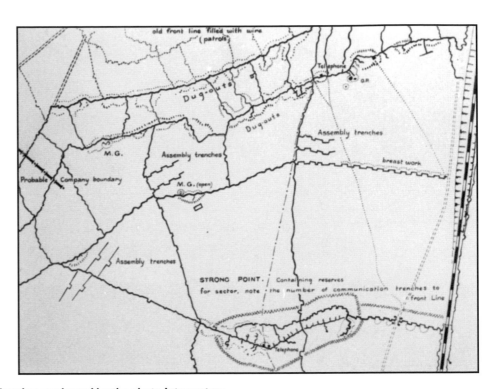

This close-up shows the trenches in Map Square 20. It is interesting to compare it to the schematic drawing prodcuced by the photo-interpreters.

It shows a section of the front line near Agny, south of Arras. From the use of German trench names, it would appear that this was compiled with the help of a captured map.

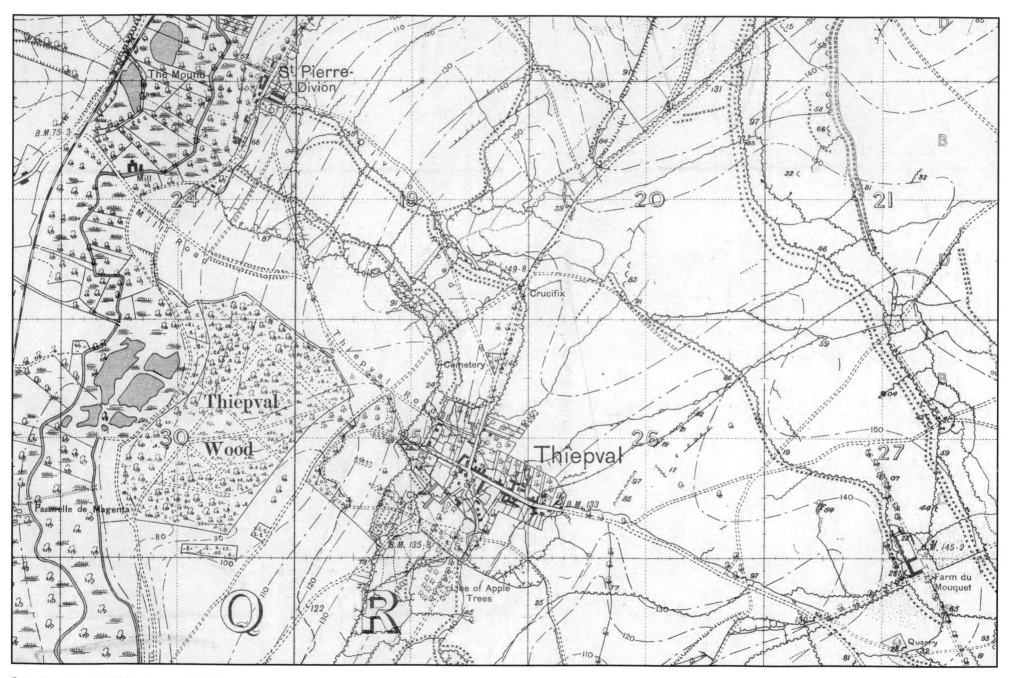

Saturday, July 1, 1916 has been called 'the blackest day in the history of the British Army'. A massive offensive of the Somme — heralded by the detonation of 18 mines under the German front line — was intended to relieve pressure on the French at Verdun; instead by evening 60,000 men lay dead and dying for virtually no gain.

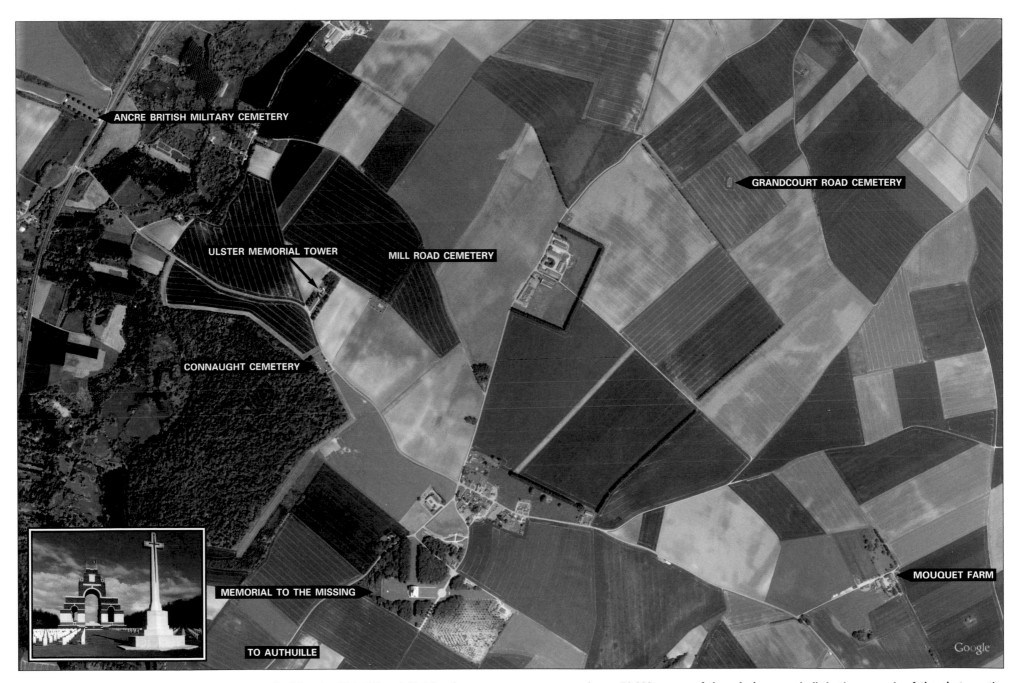

ANCRE BRITISH MILITARY CEMETERY

GRANDCOURT ROAD CEMETERY

ULSTER MEMORIAL TOWER

MILL ROAD CEMETERY

CONNAUGHT CEMETERY

MEMORIAL TO THE MISSING

MOUQUET FARM

TO AUTHUILLE

Google

At Thiepval the ruins of the chateau were attacked by the 36th (Ulster) Division in an endeavour to capture the Schwaben Redoubt. The Thiepval Memorial on which are engraved over 70,000 names of the missing, was built in the grounds of the chateau, the area finally being captured in September 1916.

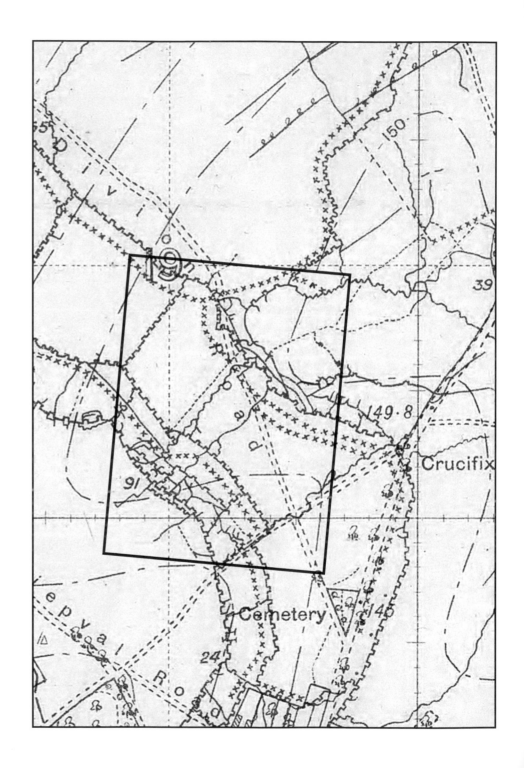

The German front line at the 'Crucifix Position' just north of Thiepval village was the area occupied by the Schwaben Redoubt. This photo was taken by No. 4 Squadron which had been formed at Farnborough in September 1912 as the unit which specialised in aerial photography throughout the war. They had the apt motto: 'To see into the future'.

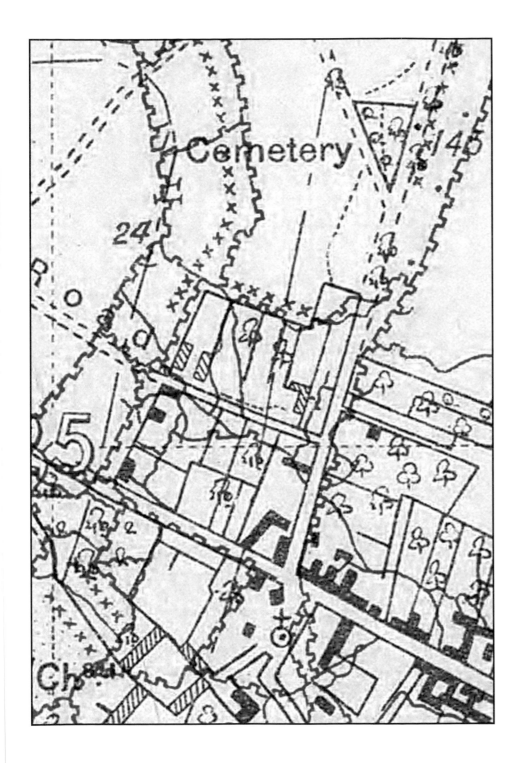

The second photograph, taken a little further to the south to encompass the village, is dated June 1, 1916 — just one month before the Battle of the Somme commenced.

Ginchy

Ginchy had already changed hands early in July 1916 and a planned assault on September 3 secured only the southern part of the village. Several further attempts were made, including a night attack on the 6th. Finally in British hands on September 9, it had cost over 4,000 casualties to capture what was by then just a pile of rubble. View taken looking north.

What was a shell-torn wasteland is now a patchwork farmland yet the tell-tale blemishes of former battles still show through even after 100 years.

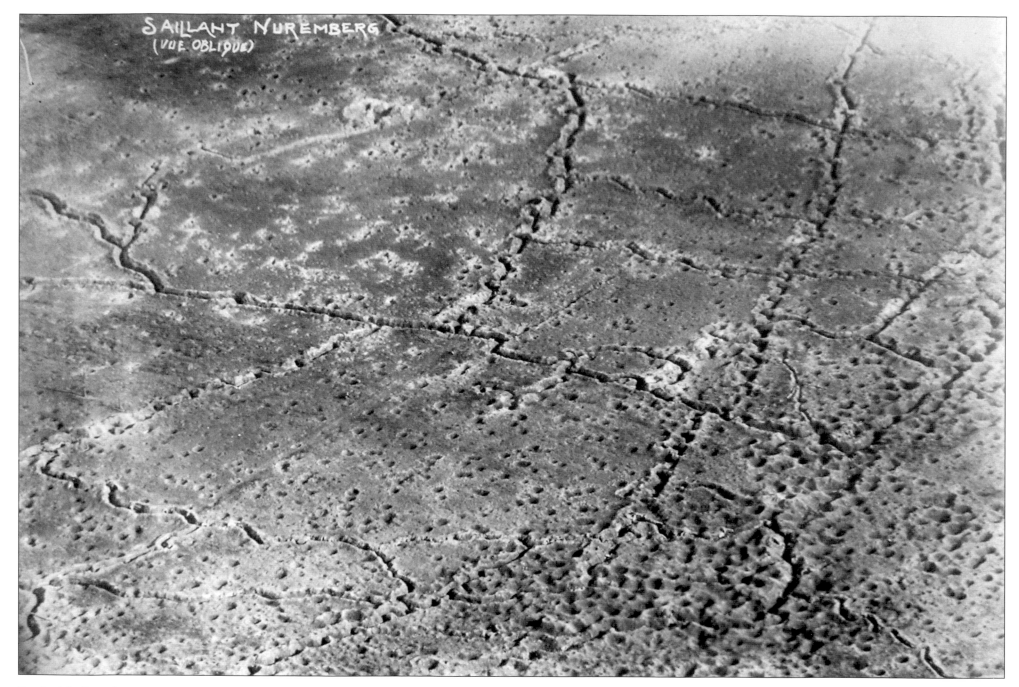

SAILLANT NUREMBERG
(VUE OBLIQUE)

South of the River Somme and just below the Amiens to St Quentin highway (the N29) lay the formidable Nuremberg Salient. This French oblique was taken looking just west of south.

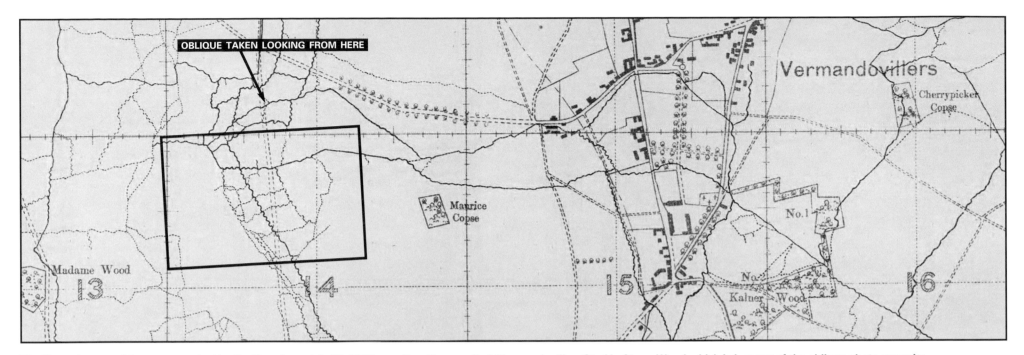

The Nuremberg position was attacked by the French on July 20, 1916 as well as the so-called 'Vermandovillers Star' in Starry Wood which is just out of the oblique photo opposite.

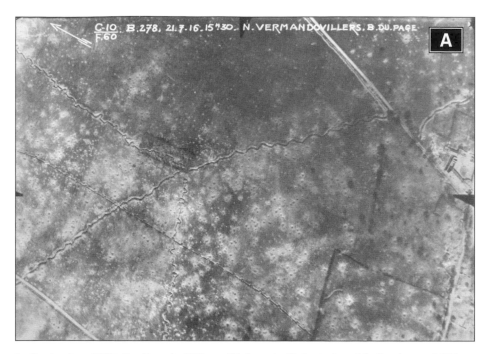

C-10. B.278. 21.7.16. 15ʰ30. N.VERMANDOVILLERS. B.DU.PAGE

A

In September 1916 the French 158ème Régiment d'Infanterie with the 1er and 31ème Bataillons de Chasseurs à Pied captured the area north of the village of Vermandovillers.

C-10. B.277. 21.7.16. 15ʰ30. VERMANDOVILLERS.

B

N29

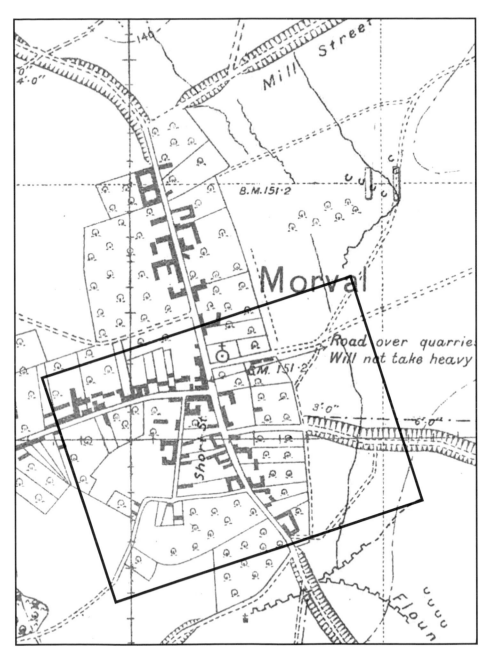

TO LESBÓEUFS

A1

TO COMBLES

The 5th Division had captured the little village of Morval, just north of Combles on September 25, 1916, just five days before the picture was taken of the shattered remains. The Germans were able to recapture Morval in their Spring Offensive of 1918 as it then lay right in the gap between two British armies, the Third and Fifth.

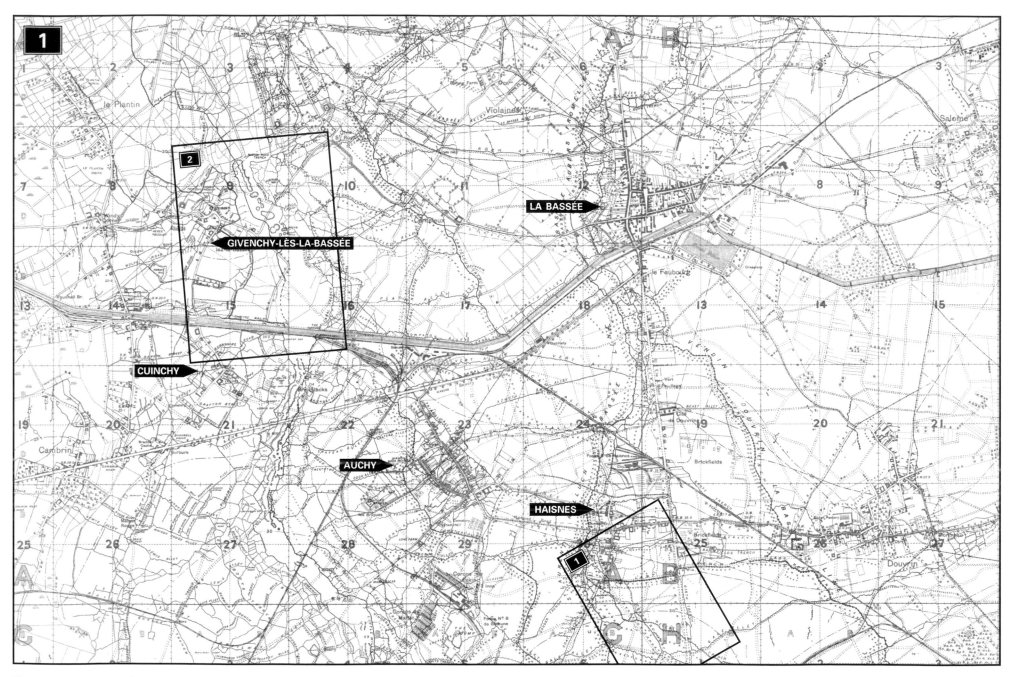

The in-depth German defences in the La Bassée area east of Béthune. The Aire Canal, which was used to serve the coalfields of the Nord and Pas-de-Calais départements, is more popularly known as the La Bassée Canal and, as this May 1918 map shows, it bisected the battlefield. (Givenchy-lès-la-Bassée must not to be confused with the Givenchy-en-Gohelle south of Lens.)

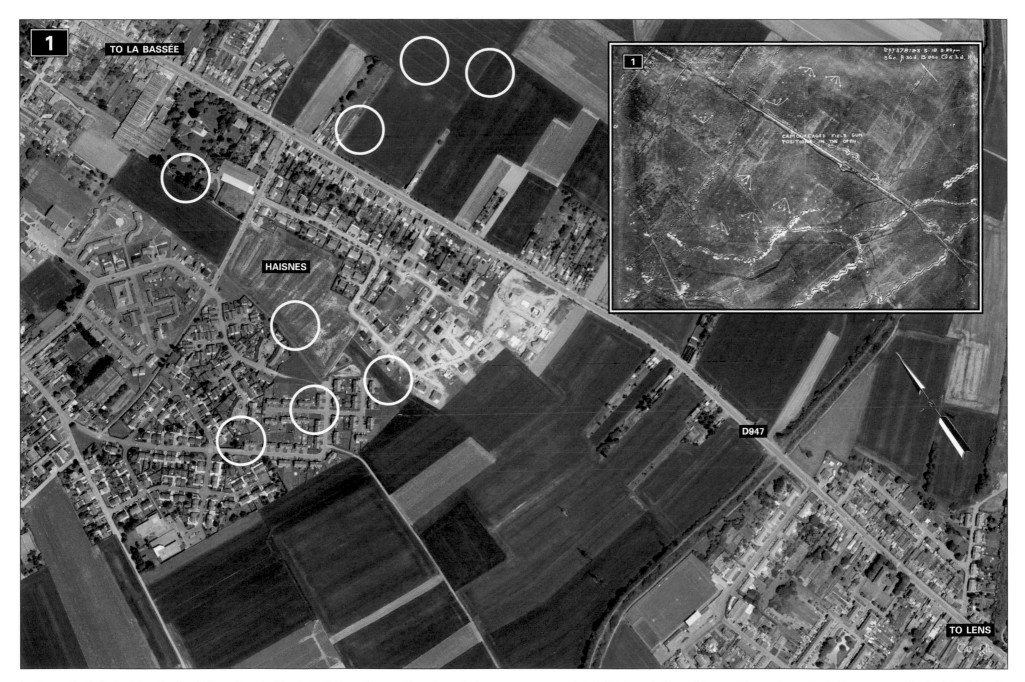

In the vertical photo taken by No. 2 Squadron in March 1918 (inset) camouflaged gun batteries straddling the La Bassée-Lens road, in Map Square 30 at Haisnes, have been annotated. We have indicated the positions where the field guns were sited with white circles on the present-day Google Earth photo.

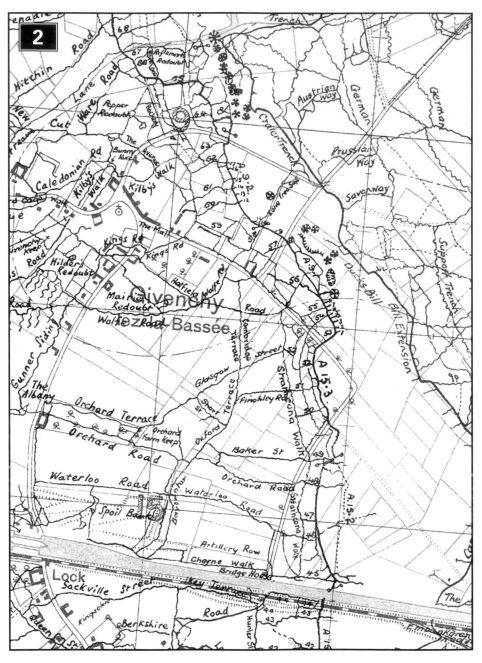

This photo, covering the British lines north of the canal, shows Givenchy-lès-la-Bassée pounded into nothingness by May 1916. Mine craters straddle the line futher north. La Bassée itself lies a couple of miles to the east. The town had been taken by the Germans at the beginning of the war and remained a heavily fortified bastion for over four years. Pounded by British artllery, little was left when it was captured just prior to the Armistice in November 1918.

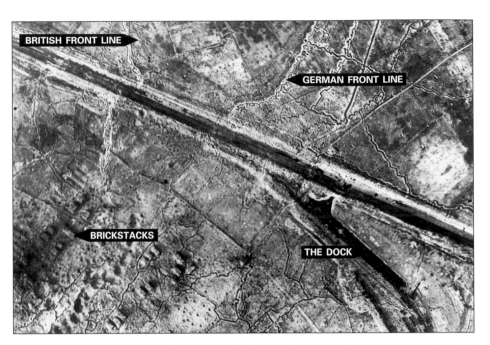

The canal split the lines, Cuinchy and the 'Brickstacks' south of the canal also suffered in the heavy fighting here in January 1915.

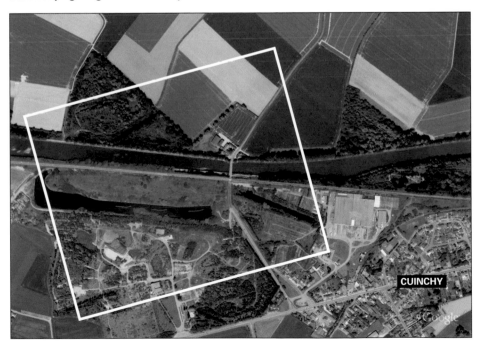

Nine villages on the Verdun battlefield which had been blasted out of existance were never rebuilt. This is Ornes which lay 12 kilometres north-east of the city.

From 1916 . . . to 2013. Nature has now claimed back what is rightfully hers, and the passing years have hidden the scars of the former battlefield.

Another of the Verdun fortresses was Tavanne (see the map on page 44).

Fort de Tavanne, six kilometres east of the city, effectively wiped from the face of the earth.

FORT DE VAUX (see page 45)

FORT DE TAVANNE

Only a faint image remains to be seen in the surrounding woodland.

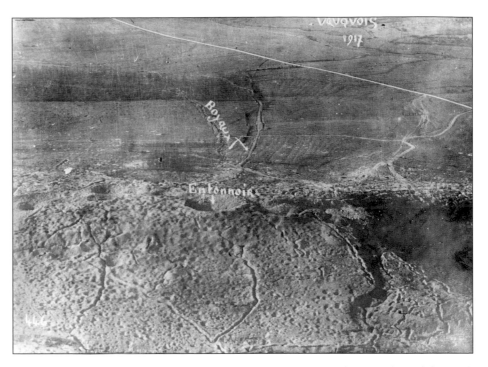

Another one of the 'lost' villages is Vaux eight kilometres north-east of Verdun and just north of Fort de Vaux (see page 45) which was battered into submission in 1916.

Vauquois, 25 kilometres west of Verdun, was blown completely from the face of the earth so that absolutely nothing remains but a series of large mine craters.

Looking north-east at the Hindenburg Line just west of Fontaine-les-Croisilles in April 1917. The dark patches are belts of barbed wire with the 'trap' entrance leading to a solid entanglement.

HÉNINEL

VIEW TAKEN LOOKING
IN THIS DIRECTION

D9

Now it is the A1 autoroute that forms an impenetrable barrier across the old battlefield. The angle of the oblique photograph and the Google Earth view is indicated on the trench map.

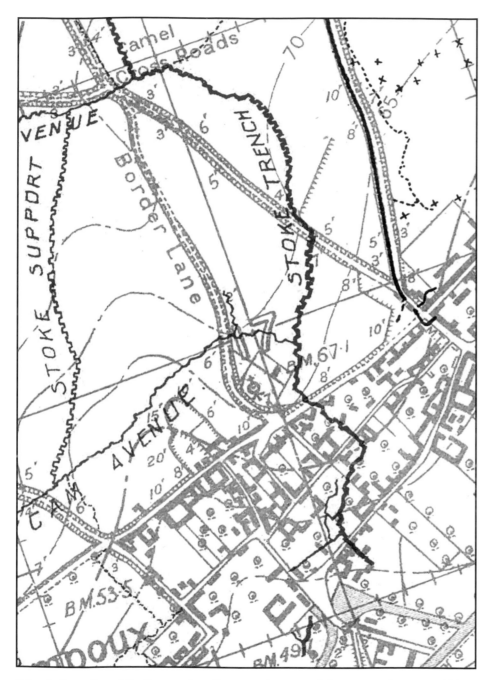

Lying in the valley of the Scarpe river, Fampoux, just east of Arras, was the scene of bitter no-holds-barred, hand-to-hand fighting. It was captured by men of the 4th Division in

April 1917, lost in March 1918 but retaken that August. This map dates from July 1918 with the British trenches now printed in red (see pages 96-97).

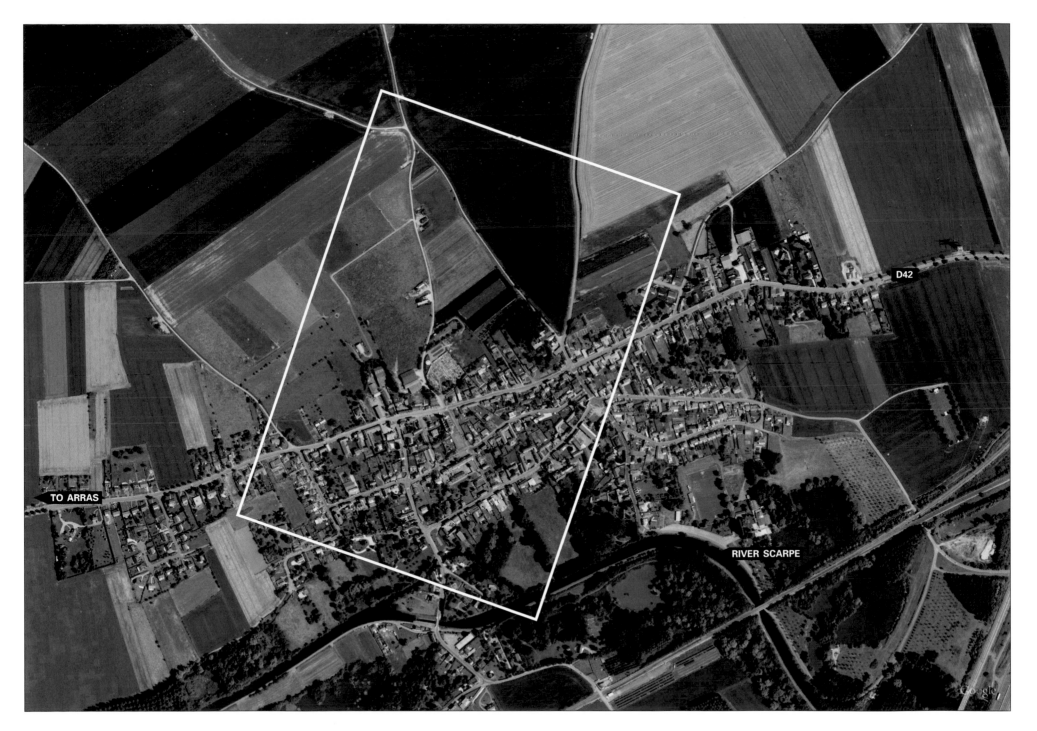

TO ARRAS

D42

RIVER SCARPE

Vimy Ridge is an escarpment five miles north-east of Arras stretching for a distance of just over four miles, crowned by the 476-foot-high Hill 145. The Germans held the ridge in October 1914 and two attempts were made by the French to capture the high ground in May and September 1915. Both sides entered into extensive tunnelling operations and the Germans exploded 20 mines in the sector so that by 1917 there were 19 distinct groups of craters. This photo montage shows the Canadian 3rd and 4th Division's front as of March 24, 1917.

The Canadian Corps took over responsibility for Vimy in October 1916 and carefully formulated a plan for the capture of the ridge. The operation began on March 20, 1917 with the main assault commencing on April 9. Three days later the Canadians had taken the ridge but had suffered over 10,000 casualties in the process of whom 3,598 had been killed. Four Victoria Crosses were awarded for bravery in the battle which was to become a symbol of Canada 'coming of age as a nation'.

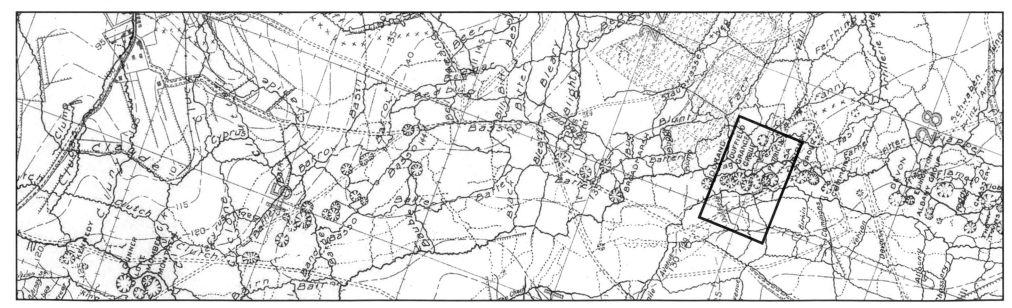

GIVENCHY

MEMORIAL

PRESERVED TRENCHES

GIVENCHY ROAD CANADIAN CEMETERY

CANADIAN CEMETERY No. 2

In 1922 France gave Canada 250 acres of the battlefield to be preserved as a national memorial and it was here that the Canada National Vimy Memorial was unveiled in 1936.

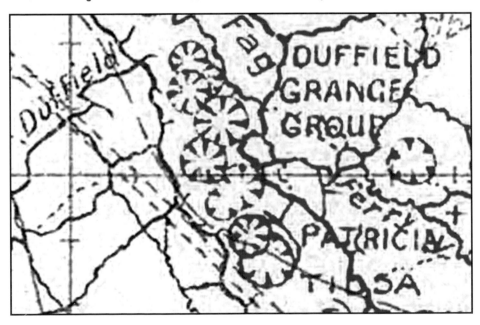

A section of the Canadian and German cratered front line has been preserved.

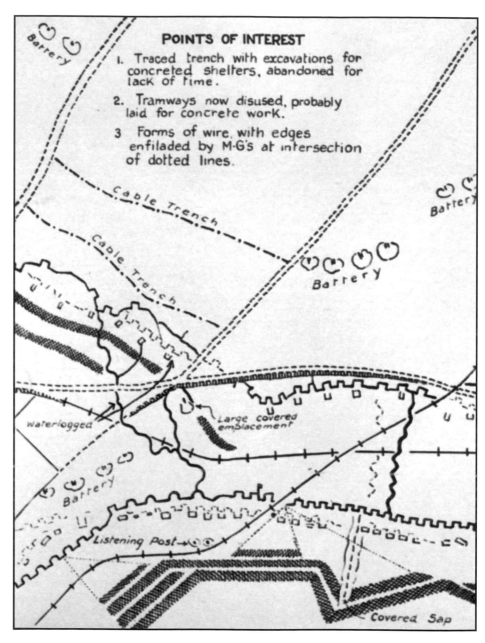

In the now peaceful fields surrounding Bullecourt and Riencourt, 10,000 Australians were killed in an attempt to breach the Hindenburg Line in 1917. On April 11, the 4th Australian Division advanced from the south-west behind 12 tanks which were soon eliminated by direct hits or breakdowns. By 2 p.m. the division had suffered 3,000 killed and over 1,100 taken prisoner. Three weeks later a second attempt was mounted by the 2nd Australian Division and 62nd British Division, the men having to advance across the corpses trapped in the barbed-wire entanglements from the earlier attack. By the time Bullecourt was secured the Australians had lost another 7,500 men and the British 6,800. Here a small section of the Hindenburg Line has been photographed and analysed to provide intelligence for the attack. Note the thick belts of wire at the bottom.

Here at Bullecourt we have overlaid the trench map on top of the Google Earth view.

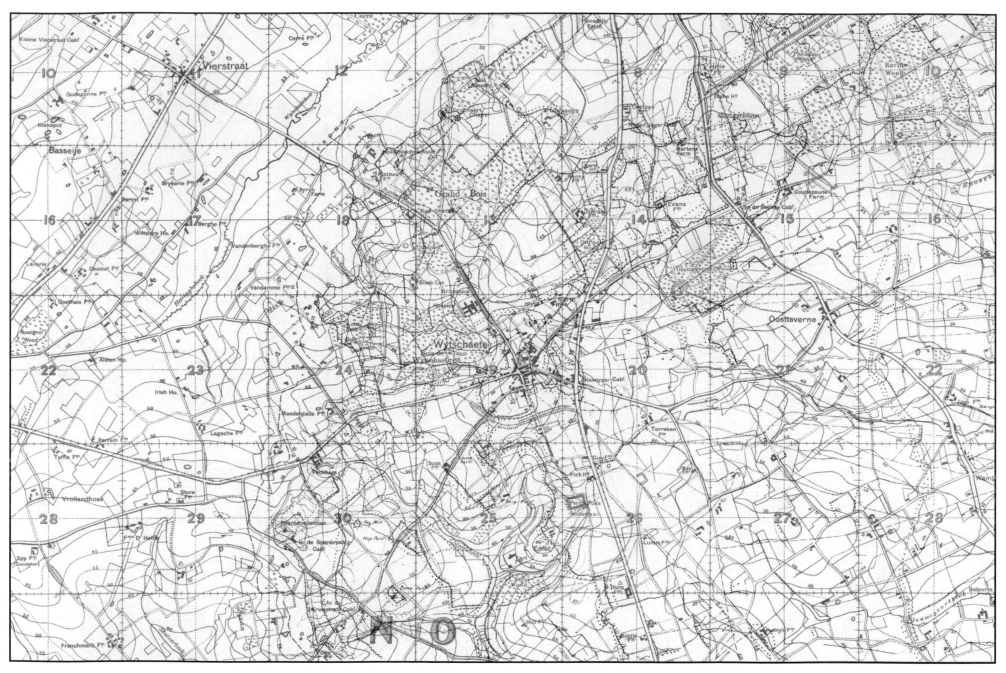

The German 'Spring Offensive' opened on March 21, 1918 and within days it threatened to split the Btitish and French forces. Swift action had to be taken to prevent a breakthrough at the junction of the British and French armies so Maréchal Ferdinand Foch was appointed to co-ordinate the Allied response, later confirmed as the Supreme Commander of the Allied Armies.

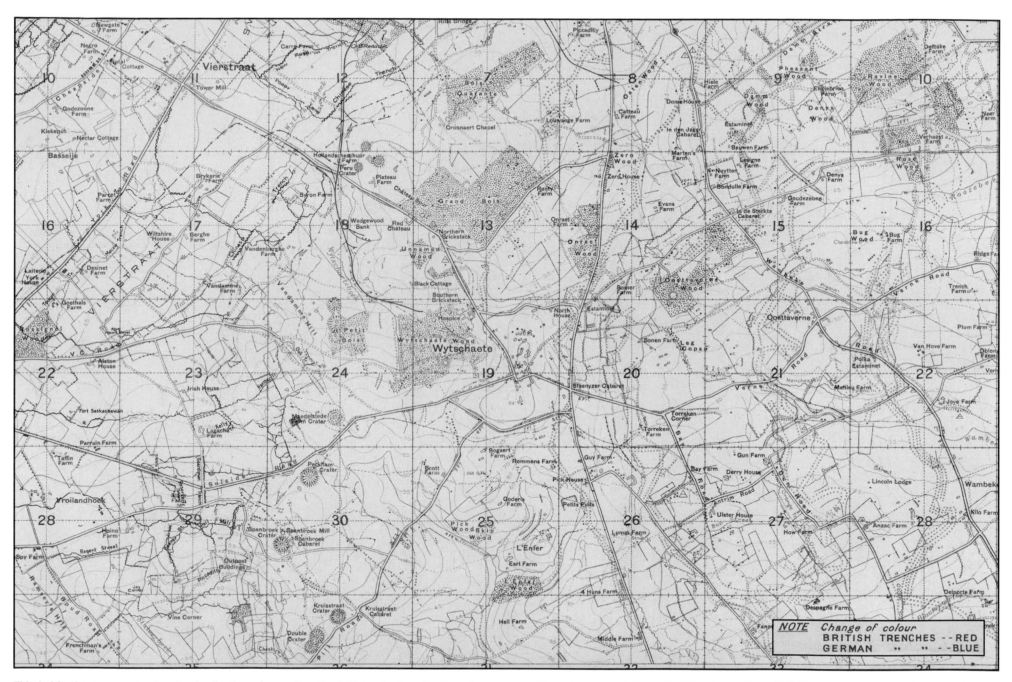

NOTE Change of colour
BRITISH TRENCHES --RED
GERMAN " " --BLUE

This led in the summer to the standardisation of mapping, the British adopting the French colour system where German trenches were coloured blue, not red as on British maps.

These two extracts from the Wytschaete Sheet 28 S.W.2 show the changes between the map produced in October 1916 *(opposite)* and September 1918 *(above)*.

The town of Wytschaete (in the centre of the maps on the previous pages) was completely decimated by 1918. The town changed hands at least three times in 1914 before the Germans held and fortified it. It was taken by the 11th (Irish) and 36th (Ulster) Divisions in June 1917 but lost in the German Spring Offensive. It was not recaptured again until September that year.

TO YPRES

WYTSCHAETE CEMETERY

N365

TO KEMMEL

TO MESSINES

Wytschaete was one of the places visited by Hitler during the tour he undertook after the fall of France in 1940 to explore the places he knew from his service in the First War. The position of the town on high ground led to its strategic importance. The memorial to the 16th (Irish) Division stands beside Wytschaete Cemetery where over 1,000 Commonwealth troops lie buried.

Not far to the west lies Wambeke Road (Map Squares 15 and 21 on the map on page 97) — a cratered landscape stretching right across the German positions just east of Oosttaverne Wood.

In this photo taken in September 1918 the village, which lay at the crossroads lower right, has completely disappeared.

Now rebuilt, the N336 leads north-west towards Ypres. The Oosttaverne Wood Cemetery can be seen in the top left-hand corner. Here lie 1,119 commonwealth soldiers of whom 783 are unknown. There is a single German grave and British and French graves from the Second World War.

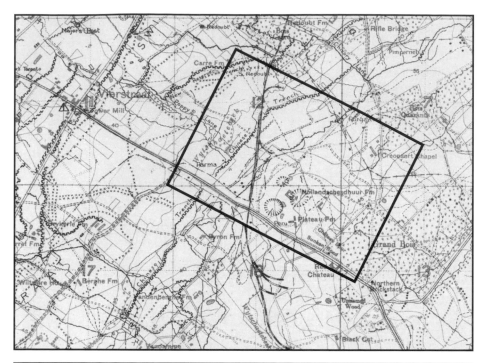

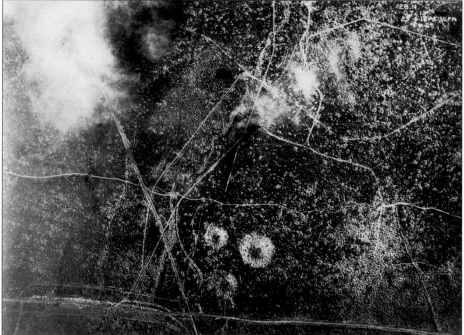

While men were killed in their thousands, striving to gain advances of mere yards, below ground another form of warfare was being fought by the tunnellers. To try to alleviate the awful casualties on the surface, extensive tunnels were dug beneath the opposing lines and packed with explosives to be detonated at the beginning of an assault. After two years' work, a chain of 24 huge mines had been prepared for a British assault on the Messines Ridge. They were fired at 3.10 a.m. on June 7, the effect of the massive explosion even being felt in England. *Left:* Three mines were laid by the 250th Tunnelling Company beneath the Hollandsche Schuur Farm alongside the N331 from Wytschaete to Poperinge, south-east of Vierstraat. *Above:* Like all old soldiers the tunnellers have faded away . . . the trench lines filled in . . . and the railway dismantled . . . but the legacy of June 1917 lives on through the water-filled craters surrounding the rebuilt farm today.

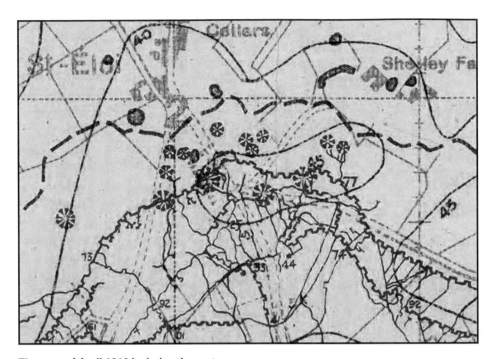

The map of April 1916 includes the craters.

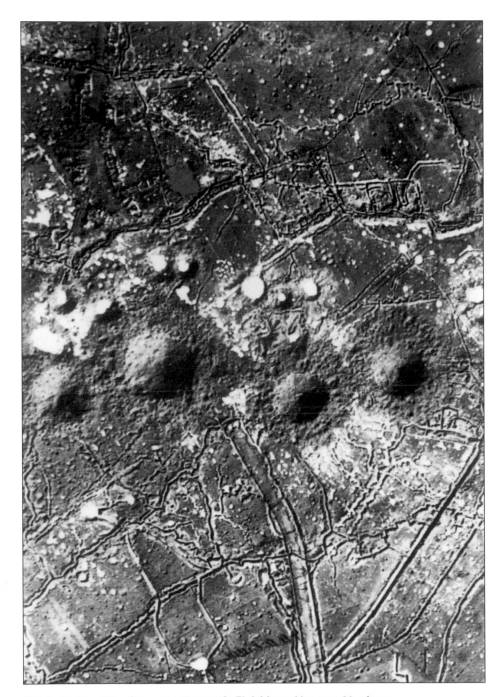

This is the tip of the German salient at St Eloi, blasted by over 30 mines.

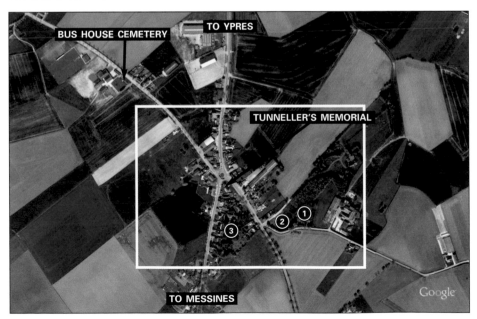

Mines [1] and [2] were exploded on March 27, 1916 and [3] on June 7, 1917.

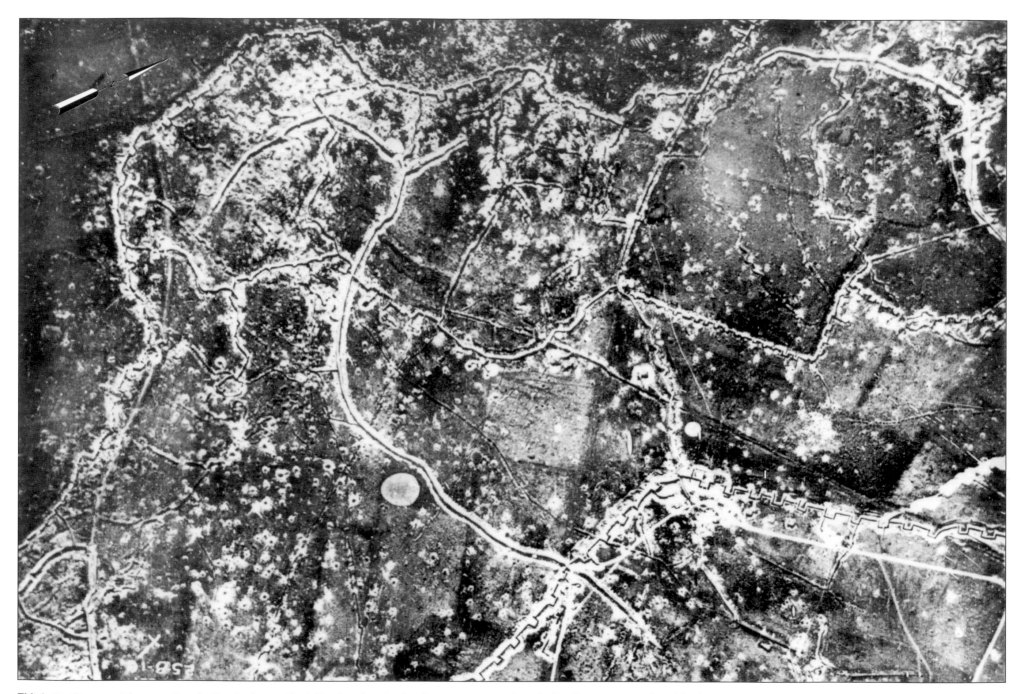

This is the German defence system further to the south at Spanbroekmolen but for some reason the print has been annotated upside down so we have turned it around so that north is at the top.

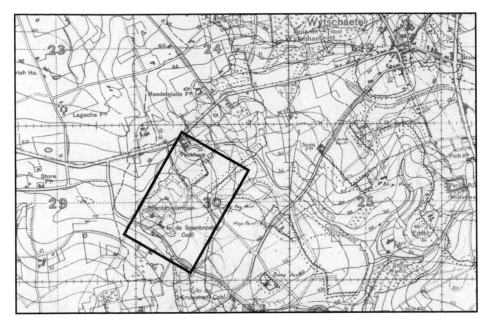

This map from 1916 shows exactly the same area as on the photograph *(oposite)*. Now from the 1918 map *(below)* we can see the line of mine craters.

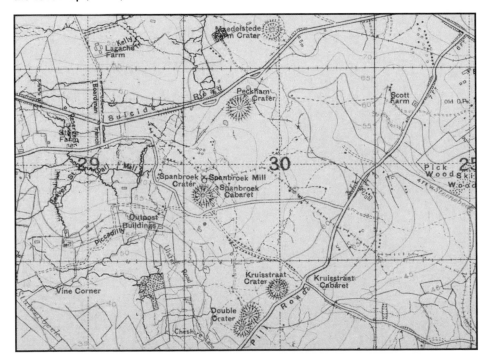

The Google Earth view shows five of the craters, the one at Kruisstraat having been filled in. The tiny Spanbroekmolen British Cemetery contains casualties from the Battle of Messines but the graves were lost during the subsequent fighting and only discovered again after the Armistice.

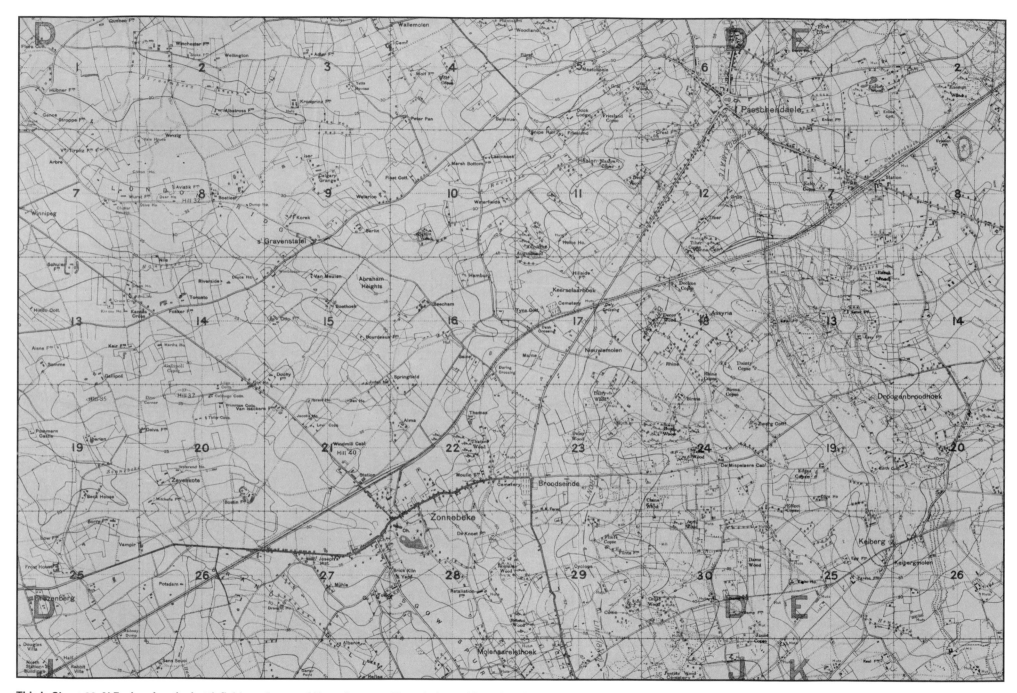

This is Sheet 28. N.E. showing the battlefield north-east of Ypres between Zonnebeke and Passchendae

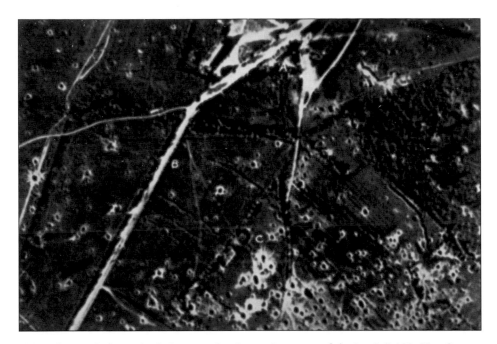

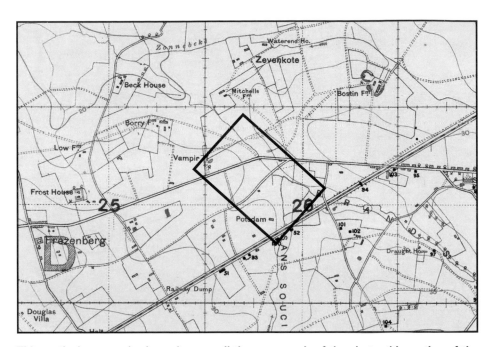

This before and after pair of photographs shows the corner of the battlefield in Map Square 26. The one above was taken on July 6, 1917 showing a dressing station on the Frezenberg-Zonnebeke road; that below after the bombardment.

This particular example shows how small the coverage is of the photo, this section of the map being from the lower left corner of the Zonnebeke sheet. The Google Earth image below shows how the sharp bend has been smoothed out.

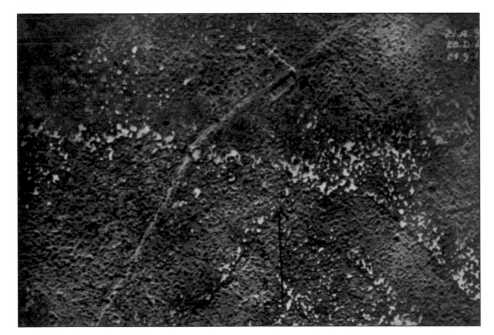

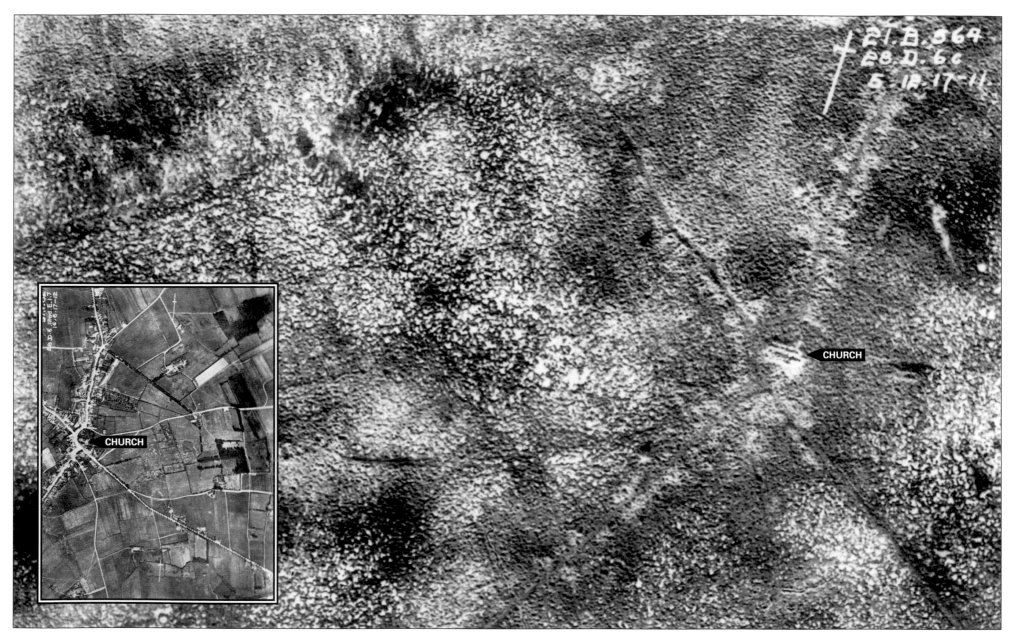

CHURCH

CHURCH

On the north-eastern corner of the map on page 106 lies the small Belgian village whose name would in future years become synonymous with slaughter — Passchendaele. The inset photo was taken in June 1917. The battle for its capture began on October 30 that year when Canadian troops, supported by the London Territorials and the Royal Navy Division, opened the assault which was technically part of the Third Battle of Ypres.

This had begun at the end of July and had continued for three months through a series of battles: Alkem Ridge, Gheluvelt, Langemarck, Menin Road, Polygon Wood, Broodseinde and Poelkapelle. On November 6 the Canadians finally reached their goal but by then Passchendaele had been pounded into a pile of rubble surrounded by miles of overlapping shell-holes in the Flanders mud. The cost of the whole campaign was half-a-million lives lost.

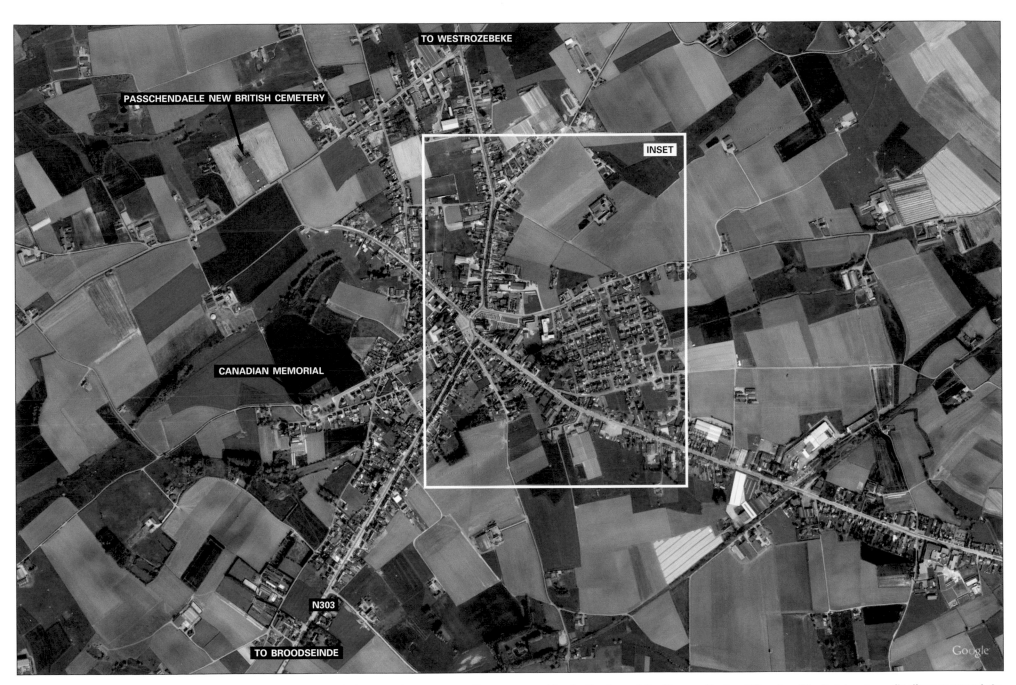

The Germans held the strategic ridge on which the village stands for over three years until the Canadians captured it but in April 1918 the Allies had to relinquish their hold on the ridge in the face of the German Spring Offensive. The Belgian Army finally recaptured the territory in October 1918.

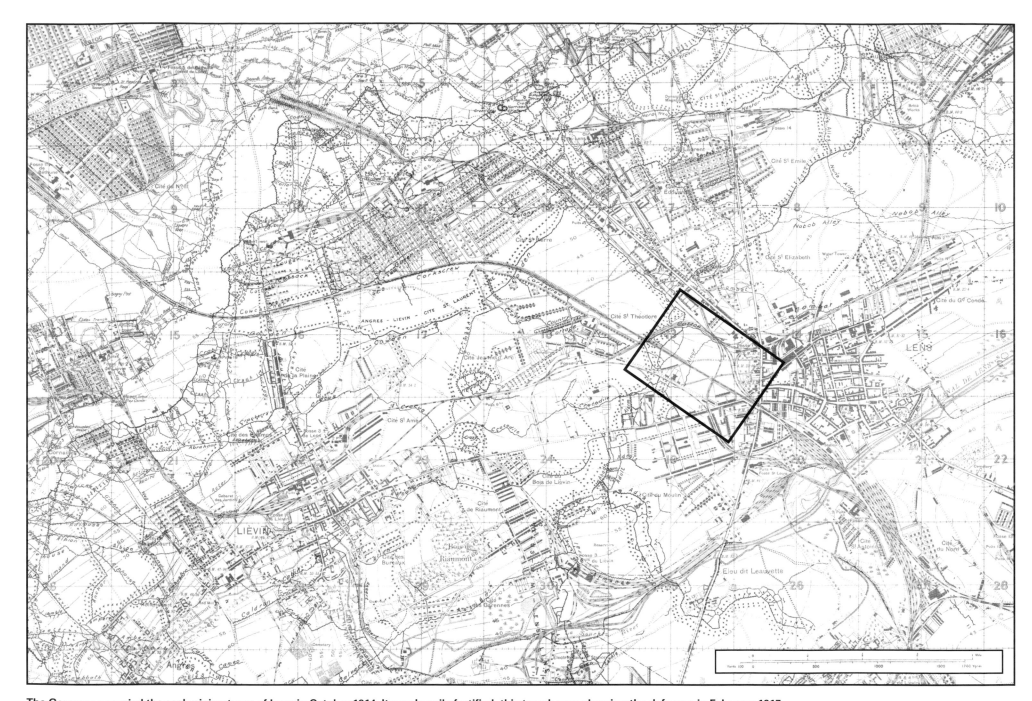

The Germans occupied the coal-mining town of Lens in October 1914. It was heavily fortified, this trench map showing the defences in February 1917.

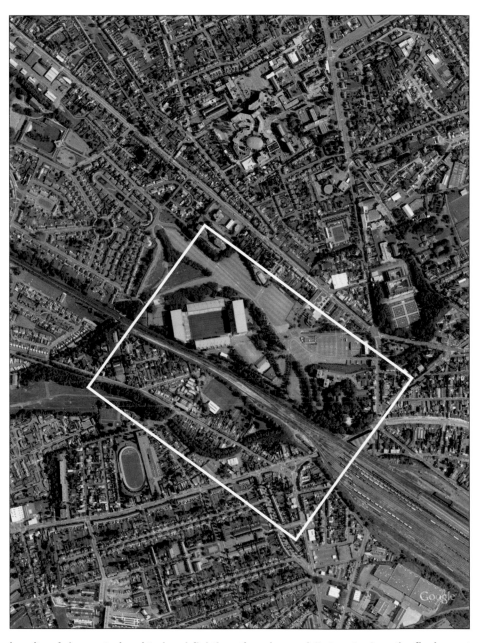

This Canadian photo, taken two months later, focuses on the rear area centred on the important railway line from the marshalling yards. The operation to capture the town was preceeded by an assault on Hill 70 to the north (off the map) on August 15, 1917. Gas shells were fired by both sides, the Royal Engineers also launching drums of burning oil and the Germans employing flame-throwers. The attack on Lens itself began on August 21 but, in spite of desparate hand-to-hand fighting, the advance failed and when the final count was made, over 9,000 Canadians had been killed, wounded or made prisoner. It was not until the end of the war was in sight that Lens was finally captured. There is little trace of the war in the thriving industrial town today, this area having been transformed with the Felix Bollaert Stadium of Lens Football Club now occupying the entrenched area.

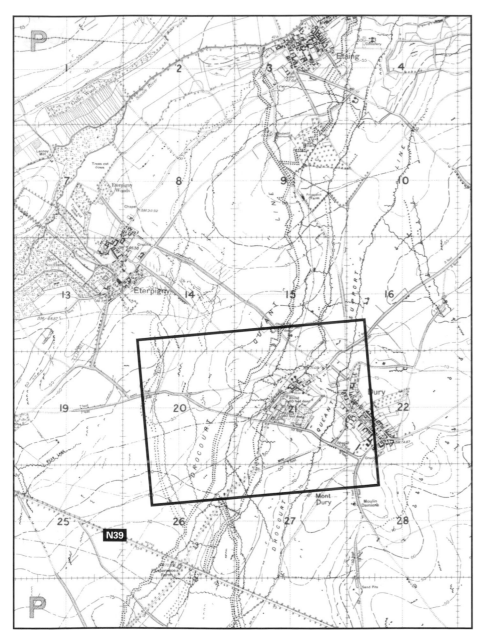

Dury lies just north of the Route Nationale 39 (since downgraded to the D939) running east from Arras. In September 1917, when the RFC took the photo *(above right)*, it was deemed a 'back area' yet it was here exactly a year later that the Canadians finally broke and turned the defences that linked the Hindenburg Line with the old Geman front south of Loos on September 2, 1918.

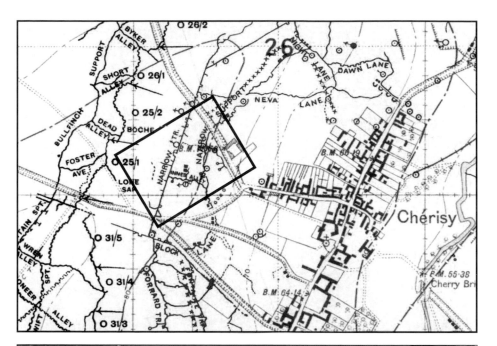

Chérisy lies over on the south side of the N39 as it then was. This photo from September 15, 1917 is a graphic example of a landscape torn to pieces by a million shells. We are looking at the German front line with the village out of the picture to the right.

What was left of Chérisy was captured by the 18th Division on May 3, 1917 but lost the same night. It then remained in German hands for over a year until the Canadians took it back in August 1918.

113

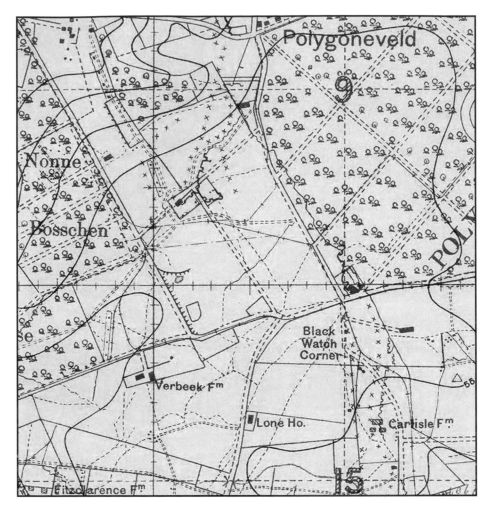

Above: **Black Watch Corner in June 1917; pulverised to nothing by September** *(below).*

As the war went on, so later editions of maps incorporated significant historical features marking particular events or battles. This is one example. The heaviest bombardment so far experienced by British forces on the Western Front took place on November 11, 1914. Shelling began at 6.30 a.m. and when it ceased at 9 a.m. the Prussian Guard attacked the Royal Highland Regiment and the Cameron Highlanders dug in at the south-western corner of Polygon Wood. Before the war, this had been the location of the Ypres Military Riding School and on October 14, 1914 the Northumberland Hussars had been the first Territorial unit to see action here. Verbeek Farm was the headquarters of the two Highland regiments but it fell to the enemy in the desparate battle on November 11. Later that afternoon, three companies from the 1st Northamptonshire Regiment, assisted by a party of The Black Watch and Camerons, advanced from Nonnebosschen Wood and retook the farm, this location later being marked on all maps as 'Black Watch Corner'. Polygon Wood was lost in May 1915 when the Germans overran it during a gas attack and it was not back in Allied hands until September 26, 1917 when the 5th Australian Division captured the wood. Their memorial stands in Buttes New British Cemetery. Subsequently the position had to be abandoned but it was finally retaken by the 9th (Scottish) Division on September 28, 1918.

POLYGON WOOD CEMETERY

BUTTES NEW BRITISH CEMETERY AND NEW ZEALAND MEMORIAL

A19

MAP

POLYGON WOOD

PHOTO

BLACK WATCH CORNER

VERBEEK FARM

Today Black Watch Corner is separated from Polygon Wood by the swathe cut acrosss the battlefield by the A19 Kortrijk to Veurne motorway.

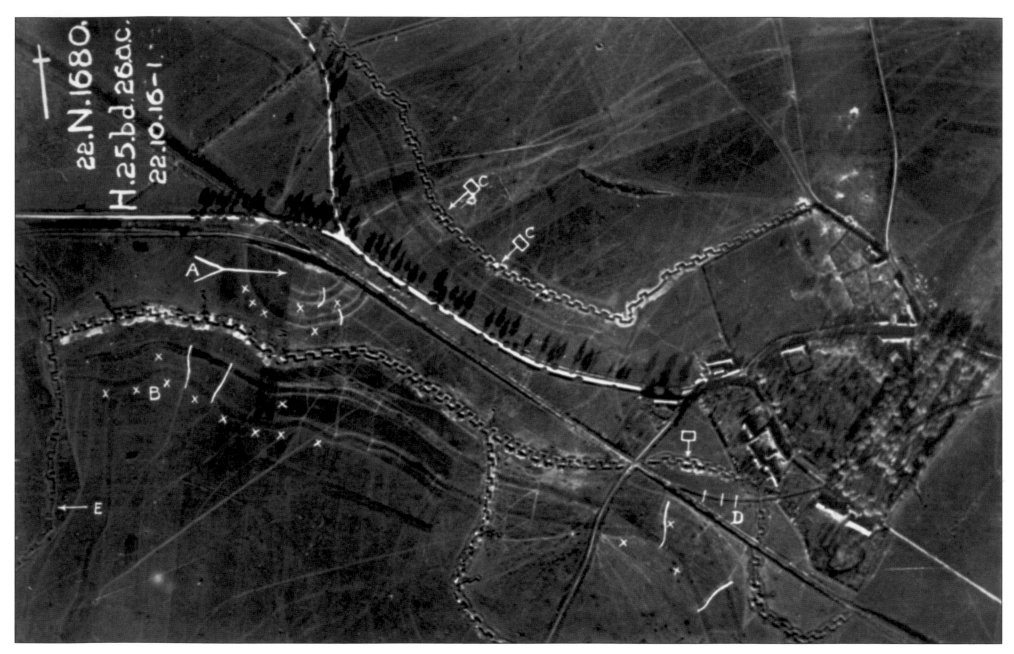

Bapaume remained in German hands from 1914 to 1917 when it was captured in March by the Australians. Lost again in March 1918, it was the New Zealanders who took it back at the end of August. This photo taken in October 1916 focuses on fortifications just outside Avenes — then a separate village just to the north-west but now merged with Bapaume.

The intelligence information issued with the picture identifies a strong point at 'A' which is given away by the wire defences. 'B' shows one of the many passages through the wire defending the position. 'C' shows one of many dugouts in a reserve trench. A railway is shown at 'D' and 'E' shows trenches marked out but not dug.

N17

N30

BAPAUME

D929

Avesnes
-les-Bapaume

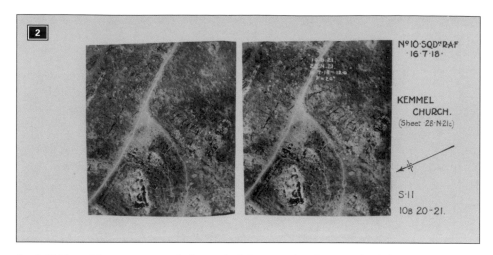

West of Wytschaete lies Kemmel and No. 10 Squadron took these stereoscopic views of the camp [1] and church [2] in July 1918. The Germans had captured Kemmel from the French in

April 1918 and it was not until the end of August that it came back into Allied hands through the combined efforts of the US 27th Division and the British 34th Division.

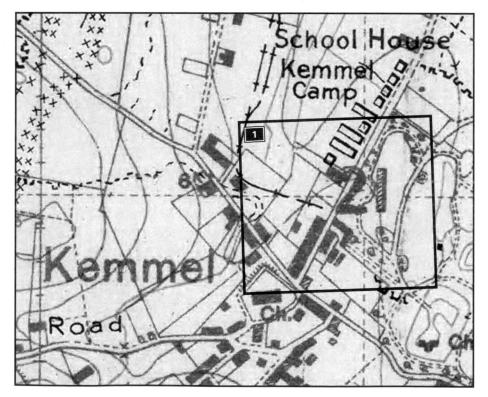

The camp. Note that we are now on the late-war maps where the German defences are depicted in blue. This extract is from Kemmel Sheet 28 S.W.1 of June 1918.

The church. Kemmel village green at the bottom of the picture with its bandstand was a favourite spot for British Army concerts during lulls in the fighting.

In July 1916, the sector occupied by the French 6ème Armée lay south of the River Somme. The village of Soyécourt was attacked and captured on July 3, this picture being taken two weeks later by French reconnaissance aircraft.

Lihons lies 18 kilometers south-west of Péronne near Vermandovilles (see page 78). It was captured in August 1918 when the Battle of Amiens marked the beginning of the end, General Erich von Ludendorff stating that it saw 'the black day of the German Army in this war'.

119

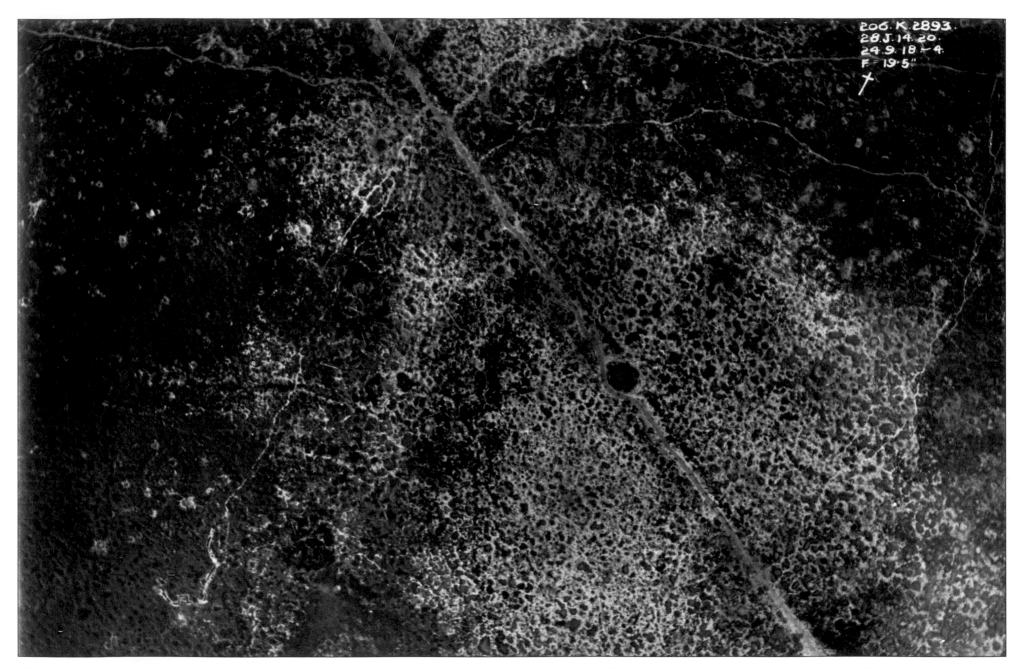

206.K.2893.
28.J.14.20.
24.9.18 ⏤ 4.
F = 19·5"

Gheluvelt stood astride the vital N8 which ran straight as a die westwards to Ypres. The village was gallantly defended in October 1914 as memorials to the South Wales Borderers and the 2nd Battalion, the Worcestershire Regiment, stand testimony, but it was not finally captured until September 28, 1918. This photo was taken four days previously by the Royal Air Force, the Royal Flying Corps and the Royal Naval Air Service having been merged into the RAF on April 1 that year.

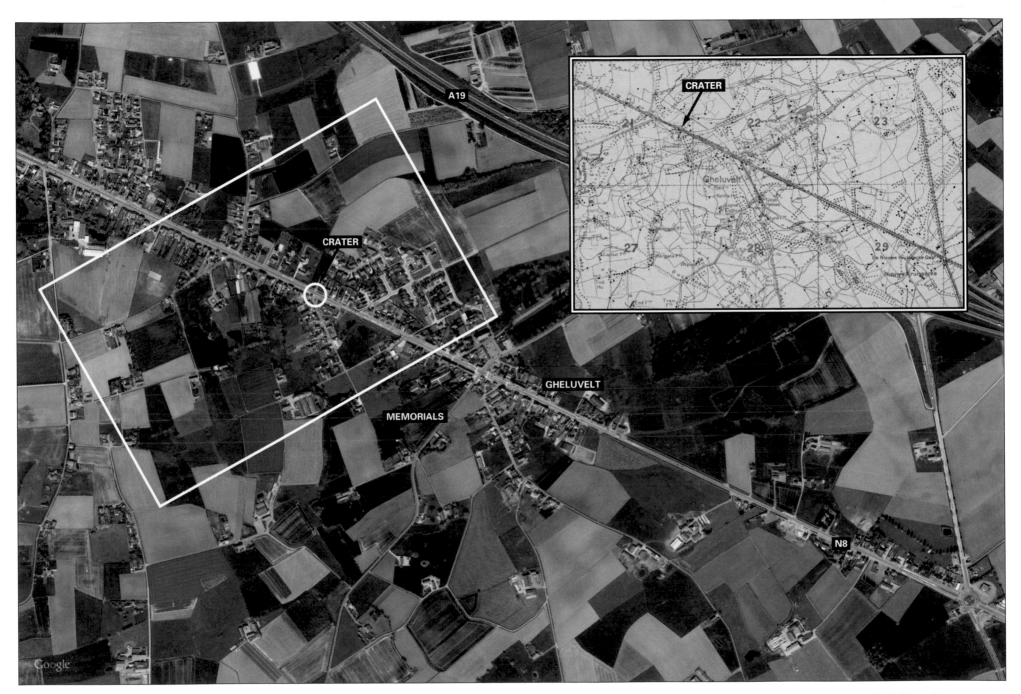

Well behind German lines, as we can see on the September 1918 map the crater has now been bypassed. The position of the memorials mentioned on the opposite page is indicated.

MALANCOURT

BOIS DE MALANCOURT

AVOCOURT

The Bois de Malancourt west of Verdun is where the French 69ème Régiment d'Infanterie was annihilated in March-April 1916. The US 79th Division also fought here in September 1918.

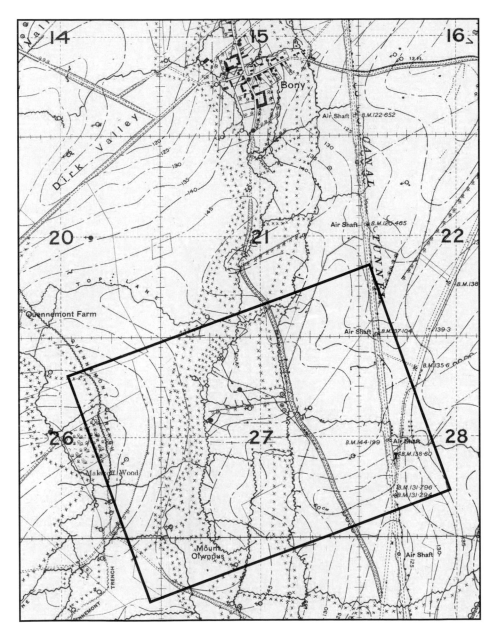

On page 65 we saw the St Quentin Canal (the Canal de l'Escaut) as part of the Hindenburg Line. The photograph shows the section of the German defence line south of Bony (north of Bellicourt) where the canal runs in a tunnel some three miles long. The tunnel was incorporated into the line by shafts leading to offices, stores, stables and hospitals with barges being used as billets. The photo and map are both from the autumn of 1917. British, Australian and American forces finally breached the line here in the autumn of 1918.

VIGNEULLES

After trying to stay out of the European war, unrestricted submarine warfare against merchant shipping finally brought the United States to declare war on Germany on April 6, 1917.

However, American troops did not begin to arrive in France until June. They were deployed south of Verdun where the St Mihiel Salient had been a thorn in the side of the Allies since the Germans broke through the French front in 1914. In September 1918, at Vigneulles-lès-Hattonchâtel, eight kilometres north-east of St Mihiel, the US 1st Division linked up with the 26th Division, thus cutting the salient in two. The village was rebuilt after the war with funds largely donated by Miss Belle Skinner from Massachusetts.

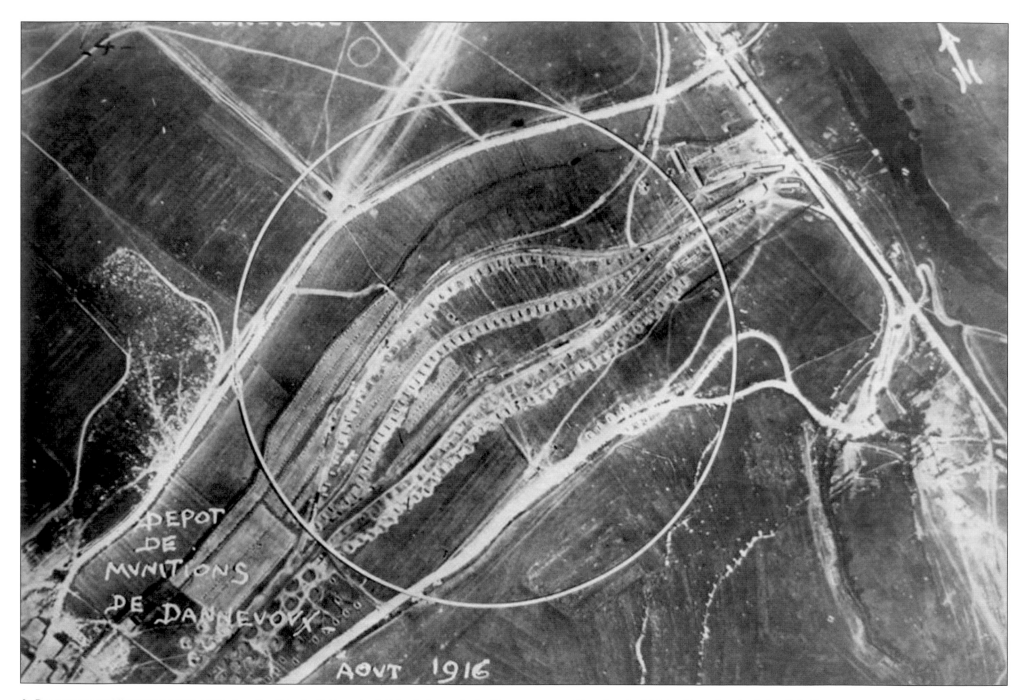

DEPOT
DE
MUNITIONS
DE DANNEVOUX

AOUT 1916

At Dannevoux, 25 kilometres north of Verdun, the French Air Force took this photograph of a German ammunition depot which had been bombed shortly before.

Nearly a hundred years have passed, and from the air, the fields of France appear to have few scars remaining as evidence of the death and destruction once wrought during the Great War.

This book has only been made possible through the dedicated service of the personnel of the Royal Flying Corps, and later the Royal Air Force, who took the aerial photographs as aeroplanes were only just coming into military use at the beginning of the Great War.

Despite this being the dawn of air combat and aerial reconnassaince, by 1918 more than 1,000 airmen had been posted missing in action on the Western Front. This is the Arras Flying Services Memorial in Faubourg-d'Amiens Cemetery which records their sacrifice.